To the poor in a rich world

This poor man cried

THE STORY OF
LARRY
WARD

NORMAN B.
ROHRER

Tyndale House
Publishers, Inc.
Wheaton, Illinois

First printing, July 1984
Library of Congress Catalog Card Number 84-50713
ISBN 0-8423-7099-4, paper
Copyright © 1984 by Norman B. Rohrer
Printed in the United States of America

contents

Wherever I am,
though far away
at the ends of the earth,
I will cry to you
for help.
PSALM 61:2

from the flyleaf of
Larry Ward's *Living Bible*

forethoughts

Few men are as strong, need less sleep, can read as fast, have traveled as many miles, have seen as much suffering, or have cultivated as many friendships in as many countries as Lawrence Edward Ward; but the theme of this book focuses on none of the above.

This is the record of a man tenanted by love, joy, and worship—a man with the courage to trust God in the paragraphs as well as in the chapters of his chartulary.

In 1957 when I met Larry in Los Angeles I knew that a treasured friend had entered my ken. That chance meeting altered the course of my life. I hope this encounter will do the same for you.

Since that meeting I have worked with him in various editorial positions, listened to him preach, read his reports about God's earth-wide enterprise, laughed at his artful and diplomatic wit, felt his shoulder-bruising welcome-home hug (a leftover from college wrestling), joined his Skippers Anonymous Club ("joggers never look like they're having fun"), watched him pray for the emaciated and dying, joined him in the halls of the mighty, and become a supporter of the relief and development projects of Food for the Hungry which he founded.

Is he perfect? Following the first interview for this book Larry wrote a note incorporating Lincoln's words to his portraitist: "Leave the warts in." Larry is sometimes criticized by judgmental Americans for his metabolism which has turned thickset into paunchy. He can sing off key, detests mice, suffers from loneliness when absent from his wife and children, can be angered by the tyranny of little minds or by an associate who dismisses a problem as insoluble, and fears taking credit for godsends.

Larry's affirmations come not alone from his peers, or from a book, but rather from the impoverished of the world whom God delivered because, as did the psalmist, this man cried and God heard him and delivered many out of all their troubles.

Dietrich Bonhoeffer described Jesus Christ as "the man for others." I think of Larry Ward, the Lord's servant, in corresponding terms.

Norman B. Rohrer

introduction
ANYONE CAN

The most self-reliant, dependable person is the one who relies upon God and lives in complete dependence upon him.

The subject of this book is such a person. Larry Ward is not a household name. He is an ordinary person in many ways. Many of the events of his life have been extraordinary (not everybody runs across a battlefield with bullets kicking up dust at his heels or sits in a presidential palace with someone who has the lives of millions in his hand).

Yes, Larry Ward is an ordinary person with some ordinary gifts. But that is precisely why this story is so very important. It is proof that anyone can be used of God, can witness miracles in his life and in the lives of others if he or she is willing to cry out to God for help and guidance, to trust God completely and to obey him.

This story about an ordinary person becomes an extraordinary book because it shows a living God in action. It is the story of how a "poor man" cried and the Lord himself heard and answered—often in unusual ways and in unusual places.

Larry Ward, one of the most effective communicators I know and one of the most compassionate, remembers that there is a *Lord* of the harvest. This frees his life of friction, of sleeplessness, and of dust; it fosters total trust even when things don't seem to go with a swing.

Like the subject of this book, you will be your best when Jesus Christ is your Lord and when your days are ordered according to his will. When you cry to him the Lord will hear and respond.

It has been sheer pleasure to know Larry. Whenever there is a cry for help around the world, Larry is there despite danger, Communist tyranny, or bureaucratic roadblocks. Would that our Lord would fill the earth with an army like him.

Pat Robertson, President
Christian Broadcasting Network

one
A DIFFERENT WORLD

Overhead a silver jet sweeps low, guns chattering, and then the long tongue of its rocket reaches out to strike the earth with violent impact. From the ground the smoke of the burning Vietnamese village snakes its dark path upward.

Standing in the midst of the rubble, the man shakes his head as if bewildered. All around him are the tragically familiar scenes of war—shattered buildings, frightened children, the bodies of the dead frozen in the grotesque positions which come from violent death. His ears ring with a clamor of desperate voices, the staccato sounds of small arms fire, the steady thump of the mortars.

Slowly the man lifts his face toward the blue sky overhead. "Father," he says aloud, grinding out each word in deep earnestness, "why—*why* have you brought me here? There's so little I can do. Why?"

He stands for a moment as if waiting for an answer. Then, as he slowly lowers his eyes, he sees something on the ground in front of him. As he bends down to pick up the mud-stained and half-burned Bible, his quickening heartbeat already tells him that here in the mud and ashes is God's answer to his cry. . . .

Suitcase in one hand and briefcase in the other, he stands indecisively in the confusion of the Dhaka airport arrival area. Naked children on all sides thrust pleading hands into his face, *lungyi*-clad porters reach insistently for his bags, loud-voiced drivers call and beckon from nearby bicycle-powered rickshaws.

As the man looks at his watch, his hesitant mind poses a question in the form of a prayer. "Father," his heart cries out, "I came here to Bangladesh because I thought you were leading me here. But maybe I should just turn around and go back to Calcutta. I don't know what to do, don't even know where to start. Please, dear God, show me what to do!"

A few hours later, in the home of the president of Bangladesh, the man prays again—this time a joyful and grateful prayer that sings in the depths of his heart. "Thank you, Father, thank you! Now I at last begin to see what you want us to do here. . . ."

Eyes lowered, he stands in self-conscious stiffness while His Royal Highness Prince Peter of Greece and Denmark pins the colorful ribbon on his chest. The ornate hotel dining room bursts into sudden applause as the Prince concludes his remarks, ". . . for furthering the cause of peace and international understanding."

As the applause continues and guests in the room surge to their feet, the man turns slowly to face them. Stepping to the rostrum, he cries out in silent but earnest prayer. "O dear God, I want *you* to have all the glory. Please give me the words to say, to turn this whole thing upward to you."

The room quiets as he begins. "You who know our work know that everything we do is done in the name of the Lord Jesus Christ, and with the desire that people be brought to faith in him. So it is in his name, for him, that I accept this honor—and then lay it at his feet as an act of worship. . . ."

Sitting on the rude log platform, looking out in wonder at the colorful crowd sitting in the huge thatch-covered temporary auditorium, the man whispers to the missionary friend beside him. "Joe, this is incredible. There must be ten thousand people in here, and thousands more outside. Every tribe in Nagaland must be here, judging from all the different blankets, and the way they are separated into so many language groups for the interpretations. . . ."

He breaks off as he hears his name being called from the rostrum. As he walks toward the pulpit, he is praying. "Father, these people have come with such expectancy. Some of them have walked for days, just to hear your Word. Use me, dear God. I cry out to you. Please. Don't let them be disappointed. . . ."

Alone in the room, he's in his shirtsleeves, pecking away at the small portable typewriter in the center of his desk. Impatiently, he pulls the sheet of typing paper from the machine, wads it up, and tosses it toward the nearby wastepaper basket.

Inserting another sheet of paper, he sits for a moment as if lost in thought. Then he bends forward, eyes closed, and buries his face in his hands.

"Dear God," he prays, "you know how the needs broke my heart there. *Please* help me to tell it now so that others will feel it as I did, and want to do something about it."

He sits for a moment, head still bowed, and then prays again: "O dear God—take me back there again, right now. Let me feel it, smell it, ache it as I did out there. Help me write it so others will care."

Suddenly he sits erect and begins to type. . . .

Scenes like those sketched in the vignettes above are commonplace occurrences in the life of Larry Ward. For a quarter of a century, logging hundreds of thousands of air miles each year (about eleven million miles in all), he has circled the globe again and again on a tireless mission of mercy.

Picture him riding through the winter night on the

"Chopin Express," the night train from Vienna to Warsaw, headed for the uncertainties of martial law in Poland.

Or see him on the deck of a rescue ship out in the South China sea, scanning the rugged waters with his binoculars, looking for that speck in the distance which may be a little Vietnamese fishing boat, carrying a frightened band of "boat people" refugees in their desperate bid for freedom.

Again, visualize him walking through the naked heartbreak of a "famine camp" in Northern Kenya . . . looking down from a tiny plane onto the earthquake-ravaged streets of a Managua or Guatemala City in the wake of sudden disaster . . . biting his lip in frustration as he watches a little girl die in Laos just because she hasn't had food enough to keep her alive and well.

Or watch him take a deep breath outside the "East Gate" in Washington, D.C., just before he enters the White House meeting which may have life and death significance for people half a world away.

And remember that in all these varied circumstances in widely different parts of the world, there is one common factor.

Larry Ward would sum it all up in one verse of Scripture which he regards as the essential thread of his life. In the words of Psalm 34:6, "This poor man cried . . . and the Lord heard him."

He's no adventurer, even though some of the chapters of his life (as related in the latter part of this book) might seem to fit a James Bond novel or CIA history.

He is quick to describe himself as "a very ordinary guy, with very ordinary abilities—but with a very extraordinary God.

"If there's one thing about my life which is worth telling," he insists to his biographer, "it's the story of the great God who has always been there to listen when I cried out to him in Jesus' name."

And then he broadens it. "I guess mine is a different kind of world from that which most people know. But this same wonderful God is available to any other 'poor man' (or woman) willing to ask his help. The greatest experiences of my life have come out of a deep personal sense of inadequacy, when I just had to cry out to him because I needed his help so much."

two
WHAT'S HE *REALLY* LIKE?

A good play needs no epilogue, and the biography of a worthy subject needs no exaggeration to heighten its appeal. Lawrence Edward Ward would be the first to acknowledge that anything worth recording about his life is held in what *The Living Bible* describes as "a perishable container" (2 Corinthians 4:7).

He quite literally agrees with the sage Ptahhotpe of the twenty-fourth century, B.C., who admonished: "Be cheerful while you are alive." Larry is almost always "up," especially early in the morning. (His wife Lorraine's evaluation: "Disgustingly cheerful; unfailingly optimistic.")

One morning in a mud hut at Bo'O, Somalia, I watched from a nearby bed as Larry got up, stretched, and greeted the day. No one else was awake, but he was already smiling broadly to himself, happy to be in that remote and impoverished refugee camp, full of energy and ready for the day's duties in dust and dirt.

With good health he is blessed, but Larry is not without physical annoyances. A bothersome rash *(lichen planus)* is probably his only outward telltale indication of reaction to deadline and diplomatic pressures through the years. An allergic reaction keeps his sinuses constantly congested,

21

especially when he is riding in a pressurized airplane cabin, which occurs about every third day.

He loves people, but hates (a) gossip, (b) quitters, and (c) excuses. A close associate says, "The only time I see him lose his temper is when someone pronounces a task or project impossible without making what Larry regards as an honest effort."

I'd add another: He can't stand to see someone slighted, whether it's a timid chum in school or a weary passenger being cut out of line by an impatient ticket holder. Once in a German airport when a passenger stepped into line ahead of the people who had been patiently waiting, Larry went up to him and said, "Excuse me, I'm from *Der Spiegel*. I'm interviewing people who cut into line ahead of others. . . ."

From his dad Larry learned the law of life: "What you do, do well." When he is concentrating on a task, such as writing an article or a TV script, he has the ability to put the rest of the world aside—in almost a self-hypnosis. Lorraine smiles in tolerant amusement when Larry—pounding away at his typewriter—will call out to her, "Lo, what time is it?" despite the watch on his wrist or the clock on a nearby wall.

Perhaps it is more accurate to say that *most* of the time she smiles. One day he apparently stretched that particular string too far. "Lo," he called without looking up, "what does your watch say?"

Lorraine looked at him with a long and icy stare. "'Tick tock,'" she replied finally and firmly. "That's what it says—'tick tock'!"

Old-time traveling companions Roy Wolfe and Hal Stack report that Larry completely unpacks every time he checks into a hotel or motel, even if just for a short overnight stay. Maybe it's because his room is his office most of the time.

Larry has a compulsion, an obsession, for neatness. "I suppose I lose a lot of valuable time," he admits, "because I just have to stop and reorganize—my desk top, my papers, my room—at regular intervals of the day and night."

In the fall of 1982 Larry enrolled for a special four-week

course at Duke University Medical School involving medical, nutritional, and psychological components. He was anxious to get competent help with his own weight control and dietary problems, particularly with the unusual (if not unique) complexities posed by his travel schedule, which takes him away 90 percent of the time. He found the psychological/behavioral aspects stimulating, felt that the nutritional studies were most valuable for his work as well as for his personal life, and was encouraged by the very thorough medical examinations he received showing heart, lungs, and vital organs exceptionally healthy for a man of fifty-seven.

On his travels, Larry constantly forgets his glasses (especially sunglasses). There is a scattering of them all over the world in airplane seat pockets, restaurant tables, hotel checkout counters, and rental cars.

His obsession about time relates to a larger principle in Larry's life. Often I heard him pray in the morning something like this: "Lord, we thank you for this day. As men measure time, here's a day we have never lived before in eternity, a day we shall never live again. Please put into it by your grace what you want it to include. Help us today to invest this gift of time wisely . . . to live this day the way we will wish we had lived it when we meet you face to face."

Perhaps that's why Larry is up and working by four o'clock most mornings—and often earlier. He needs less sleep than most and can catnap in automobiles, trains, planes, or buses at any time he wishes.

The last message Larry received from his mother focused on this element of precious time. Orleva Ward died on Christmas Day, 1957. ("How terrible," said a sympathetic nurse, "to die on Christmas." Larry smiled through his tears and replied: "Our mother would have said, 'How wonderful to meet my Lord on the day men celebrate as his birthday.'")

Larry recalls how he and his dad, brothers, and sisters, maintained a constant twenty-four-hour vigil at her bedside, talking to her and trying to coax her out of the coma into which she had suddenly slipped on his birthday, December 14. "We prayed that she would open her eyes for just a moment," Larry said, "and at least say *something* to us—some last word before she died. But she never woke up until she woke up in heaven; she never spoke until she lifted her voice in praise to God up there."

After the funeral, Larry came home to find a stack of sympathy cards mixed up with the Christmas greetings which had arrived in his absence. But in the pile was a different kind of card, and he blinked in puzzlement for a moment until he realized it was a birthday card. He had forgotten all about his birthday, during those long and trying eleven days in the hospital.

And when he opened the card to check the signature, he says, "My heart gave a kind of leap that I know you will understand. It was from my mother. Apparently the card was on its way to me while I was rushing up north to be with her. It must have been written just before she went into the coma. There was just a brief comment about the busyness of the pre-Christmas season, and then Mother added, 'This week, I must make the time count.'"

Larry italicizes those words in his thinking: *This week, I must make the time count.* "What a way," he says, "to begin one's last week of conscious life on earth. What a wonderful way to begin every week, every day."

The pressure of time leads Larry to prepare detailed time-phased worksheets for every day of his life. These probably lead him to take on more than he should, to try very often to fill the slots with more work than it is humanly possible to do.

Still, Larry's output of work is prodigious. Donald Simonsen, a member of both the U.S. and International boards of Food for the Hungry, recalls how Larry returned from a trip to Israel, spent one day at home in office conferences, and then had to leave on a trip to Asia. "During that one busy day at home," says Don, "despite jet lag and all, Larry wrote over twenty letters to the different government officials he had just contacted in Israel. He sent me copies, and each letter was different, personal."

Larry carries a little tape recorder at all times, and dictates wherever he is—even driving down a busy freeway in the States or speeding along an *autobahn* in Europe.

At airports he shaves it close, often arriving barely in time to board a plane. This practice has changed with age, but on many occasions he used to squeak into the cabin just as the door was closing.

One time Gene and Loretta Furlong drove him to Los Angeles International Airport and arrived at the check-in counter to find the plane had just left. They could see it taxiing down the runway toward takeoff position. The Furlongs saw Larry whisper something to an attendant, then start running—baggage in hand, coat and tie flying in the wind. The plane returned to the tarmack. Larry clambored up the ramp, waved once, and then was swallowed by the jet that would take him half a world away before he would step outside again.

Lorraine and Larry Ward have a deep love for the children of the world and a very special love for their own son and daughter.

"It's wonderful watching the children grow up," Lorraine observes, "but a special delight when your own children become your adult friends. In fact, Larry and I regard our Sheri and her Bill, and our Kevin and his Penni, as our closest friends. We spend our holidays together, take trips with them when we can, and get together for dinner whenever possible.

"And how we thank God," she adds, "when we see them all active in church. Larry was gone so much of the time when they were growing up, and we have seen other families which have paid a terrible price in misunderstanding and separation and spiritual bitterness. But God somehow gave Sheri and Kevin a sense of shared purpose in their daddy's work, even when they were very small."

To Larry that "somehow" is readily explained: "Lorraine accepted it as perhaps no one else could—or would. But perhaps 'accepted' is not exactly the right word. She led the kids in a very positive participation in the work. She didn't merely 'accept' it—she made it her ministry. Not that it ever was easy. I think, in fact, that it has gotten more difficult all through the years. But she turned a potential tragedy into a triumph."

If you have lots of time to spend, get Larry and Lorraine started on the subject of their grandchildren, Melissa Lorraine (Moy) and Courtnie Brooke (Ward).

"I used to think I was the 'fastest draw in the West' when it came to pulling out their pictures," admits Larry, "but somehow Lorraine always had hers out while I was still reaching. She belongs in the *Guinness Book of World Records*. By the way—have you seen our latest pictures?. . ."

Sometimes when Larry looks into the face of a starving child in some Third World famine or refugee situation, he feels that for a moment he sees Melissa or little Courtnie. He often tells about a little girl in Laos, years ago, dying before his eyes—who turned out to be almost exactly the same age as his beloved Sheri. He regards that as one of the specific incidents which led to the founding of Food for the Hungry.

Tears fill his eyes when he relates an incident involving two-year-old Melissa. She was sitting in her high chair with her cereal bowl untouched. Her spoon was motionless in the air; her little lower lip was protruding.

"Melissa," exclaimed Mommy Sheri, "what's wrong?"

Looking straight ahead, little Melissa quavered: "Some kids, no food."

To really know Larry Ward, you have to watch him with a bunch of kids. I recall an incident on the mainland of China one time at the Sun Yat Sen school where we stopped for a short visit. Larry and I picked up Ping-Pong paddles for a quick game there on the compound of Red China's prized school. Soon the youngsters were squealing with delight at the antics of this big American. His deliberate stumbles, his clever backhand shots, his feinting and thrusting, wild serves and pretended panic sent up cheers of laughter from the playground and balconies circling the arena.

High up in the mountains of Taiwan, Larry taught the Chinese-speaking kids to chant, "Hoo-ray for the Dodgers." All around the world he has taught that chant to children who may be using it even today without knowing they are rooting for a faraway Los Angeles baseball team. Anthropologists and ethnologists of future generations may have a tough time trying to figure out the origin of this chant!

Dulal Borpujari tells of a heartwarming scene in Phnom Penh, Cambodia, shortly after that country opened to the outside world. "Larry got one little child to imitate him, then another, and finally many others joined in. They would run when he did, stop when he stopped, cheer for the Dodgers when he signaled—all the time laughing their heads off. It was beautiful, but it was also deeply moving. I saw parents watching—laughing and crying at the same time. Some of them had probably never heard their children laugh before—certainly not like this. Soon about three hundred of them were following their American 'Pied Piper' down the street—until a stern-faced guard with a gun chased them away."

Karen Burton Mains dedicated her beautifully written book *The Fragile Curtain* (a compassionate look at the world of refugees) "to Larry and Lorraine Ward, and to others like them, who have seen the world in torment thousands of times and are still moved to tears."

It was a fitting description, for to travel with Larry through what he refers to as "the world of hunger" is to sense again and again the depths of his genuine compassion.

Dr. W. S. Mooneyham once introduced Larry as having "a computer for a brain, a marshmallow for a heart."

When Larry reminds us that each minute 28 people (most of them children) starve to death or die as a result of extreme malnutrition, you *know* how he feels. When he quotes the statistic that each day 40,000 people die just because they don't have food enough to keep them alive and well, he almost always quickly adds: "They die one at a time, so we can help them one at a time. *But each one is one too many.*"

The teenaged Larry Ward who dived unhesitatingly through the window of a runaway car to save a little boy's life is the same Larry Ward who today drives himself on a constant mission of mercy through the battlefields and disaster zones and famine areas of the earth—and has done so for a quarter of a century.

What keeps him going? I think Larry could honestly answer that question: "The love of Christ constrains me."

When he talks about that different kind of a world of his, tears often well up in his eyes—whether in personal conversation, speaking in a church service, or reporting on TV or radio. But Larry makes a clear distinction between emotion and compassion. He often quotes the late Bob Pierce: "Pity is something you feel. Compassion is something you *do.*"

Theologically Larry firmly holds to typical Baptist convictions. But he has deep respect for charismatic leaders such as Dr. Pat Robertson and Ben Kinchlow of TV's "700 Club." He has warm friendships with charismatic leaders such as Oral Roberts and Harald Bredesen, as well as with officials and missionaries of various Pentecostal groups.

And Larry will quietly testify to the impact of the Holy Spirit on his own life. For example: "On my first trip to Bangladesh in 1972, I was a guest in the home of Cal and Marion Olsen—missionaries of the Assemblies of God, two of the most Christlike people I know. In my room I found several books on various Pentecostal emphases and subjects such as 'the Baptism of the Holy Spirit.' Frankly, I wasn't too impressed, even though I was trying to read with an open mind. One book was by a Baptist pastor relating his experience of 'speaking in tongues,' but the scholarship was dubious.

"Finally I closed the books, and knelt to pray before going to sleep. As I did so, there suddenly flashed into my mind the words of A. B. Simpson regarding the 'gifts' of the Holy Spirit. As I recalled it, he said something like 'Seek not, shun not.' No sooner had I remembered those words when I suddenly *felt* the presence of the Holy Spirit as I had never experienced him before. Welling up within me were great surges of the soul, great paeans of praise, overwhelming feelings of worship, beyond anything I could express in words of my own. All I could do was to trust the Holy Spirit himself—'Who makes intercession for us with groanings which cannot be uttered'—to carry these deep feelings to the Father for me in the form of articulate prayer."

On another occasion Larry (in Arizona) responded to an urgent call from a friend with a great spiritual need. He rushed to a plane and flew to Sacramento to meet with her and her brother. After just a brief period of conversation, Larry looked at her and said quietly, "Are you trying to tell me that you feel you are under demonic influence or pressure?" When she nodded tearful assent, Larry instantly dropped to his knees to pray. "What happened next is too sacred to describe, except to say that God himself was suddenly in that room, and the Holy Spirit took over in prayer. When I (we?) finished praying, there was a warmth—a glow, an indescribable peace—which filled the room. All three of us felt it. None of us had to comment on it. We just knelt there and smiled at each other, in gentle and perfect understanding."

Illustrations of Larry Ward's compassion could fill several books, for this has been his driving life force through the forty years in which he has followed Christ.

Let one incident suffice here. In 1958 Larry visited the Church of the Lepers in Taiwan, with his missionary friend Lillian Dickson. In what Lil Dickson called the "Ward Nearest Heaven," Larry found a man with "a radiant testimony" for the Lord Jesus Christ. The man showed all the ravages of his disease. His skin had the leathery texture; his hands were just stumps. He was obviously blind. But the light of the gospel had reached that dark corner, and the man wanted everyone to know it. His "testimony" was simple. Whenever he sensed that someone had entered that room, he raised his right hand toward heaven.

I'll never forget Larry's description of that first encounter. "I knew what the upraised hand was saying. It said, 'Here's where my faith is based. Here's where my hope is placed.' It was his way of pointing us toward God, of inclining our thoughts toward the Savior."

Larry added: "This man wasn't doing much, by usual human standards. But he was doing all he could with what little he had. God help us to do the same."

The story has a beautiful sequel. About a year later Larry was back at the Church of the Lepers, back in the Ward Nearest Heaven. He stood again by the bedside of this man who months before had made such a deep impression on him. But now there was a difference. The man's breathing was labored, and his strength seemed almost gone.

"Look, Larry," said Lil Dickson. "He's so weak. He can't even raise his hand anymore."

But then both Lil and Larry noticed something. They looked at each other in tearful wonder as they watched the man's right hand—and saw what was left of his little finger twitch and move against the white sheet. "Why—he's trying to raise his hand again," Lil exclaimed, "but all he can do is move that little finger."

Larry and Lillian Dickson prayed for the man, and then started on to continue their rounds through the hospital. But Larry couldn't leave the room until he went over to stand by the bed once more. And once again he saw that little finger struggle to move.

Larry Ward's heart told him what to do. He reached down, carefully took that wasted hand in his own, and then—supporting the arm—gently lifted it up . . . until he saw a smile flicker across that tired face, as once more a child of God could praise his Creator with an upraised hand.

My wife Virginia and I have been with Larry in the teeming cities of Asia, in the forgotten corners of famine in Africa, in refugee centers around the world. We can bear witness that when Larry Ward saw the multitudes, he had compassion on them.

We have been there when "this poor man cried" to the Lord.

And we have also been there when he just plain cried.

three
MILESTONES

Following are some of the key events in the life of Dr. Larry Ward:

1924	December 14: born in Sidney, New York, youngest of five children of Whitney and Orleva Ward.
1940	July 11: dedicated life to Christian service. Later that same year, licensed to preach—at age fifteen.
1942	High school graduation in Norwich, New York. Honored as "one who has done the most for his school." Entered Wheaton College in September.
1943-46	In military service, doubling as Youth For Christ director in Watertown, South Dakota, while stationed at Army Air Base there. Returned to Wheaton College in September, after brief period of service with Le Tourneau Evangelistic Center in New York.
1947	July 5: married to Lorraine Alice Hustad, RN, in Hibbing, Minnesota.

1949	Graduated "with high honor" from Wheaton College; began full duties next day with *Christian Life* magazine.
1949-52	Managing editor of *Christian Life*. Daughter Sherilyn Sue born June 16, 1951.
1952-55	Director of publications, General Association of Regular Baptist Churches and editor of *Baptist Bulletin*.
1955-56	Director of educational services, Gospel Light Publications.
1956-57	First managing editor of *Christianity Today*.
1957-62	Vice President/Information Services for World Vision; first editor of *World Vision Magazine*. Began continuous world travels in August 1958—same month in which son Kevin Charles was born (August 6).
1958-65	Served as Executive Secretary of Evangelical Press Association and Director, EP News Service.
1963-64	Joined Roy Wolfe to form TELL Services as information agency assisting Christian organizations.
1965-70	Rejoined World Vision at urging of his friend and mentor Dr. Bob Pierce, becoming Vice President/Overseas Director. Had major involvement for World Vision in Vietnam (forty-four trips there in forty-eight months).
1969	Azusa Pacific College, Azusa, California, awarded him Doctor of Humanities degree; Yonsei University, Seoul, Korea, conferred Doctor of Laws degree.
1971	Became first president of Food for the Hungry International.

1972   One of first evangelical leaders to enter Bangladesh, in January. Met with president, prime minister, and U.N. officials to plan major relief airlift.

1973   Directed earthquake relief in Managua, Nicaragua.

1974   Visited famine areas of Africa's Sahel; rushed help to Honduras after Hurricane Fifi. Authored *And There Will Be Famines.*

1975   April: put first Vietnamese "boat people" in water; led "exodus" of hundreds of refugees from Saigon. Established unique "Hope Village" for 1,100 refugees in Weimar, California.

1976   In Guatemala to meet with disaster relief officials just four weeks before major earthquake; returned immediately to direct massive assistance program. In August, entered war-torn Lebanon on small refugee boat from Cypress; met Dr. Charles Malik (former President, U.N. General Assembly) to initiate relief assistance.

1977   One of first outsiders on the scene after the Romanian earthquake.

1978   Launched "Operation Rescue" mercy ship program for Vietnamese refugee boat people. Honored by His Royal Highness Prince Peter of Greece and Denmark "for furthering the cause of peace and international understanding."

1979   First visit to Vietnam since political change.

1980   Began FHI refugee assistance programs in Somalia.

1981   Established International Coordination Center for Food for the Hungry International in Geneva, Switzerland. Among three named as 1981 Wheaton College Distinguished Alumni of the Year.

1982   January: with colleague Dr. Tetsunao Yamamori, visited Poland under martial law; began major assistance program there.

1983   Saw longtime dream answered in official formation of Food for the Hungry/Japan in July; completed a major "Disaster Preparation Checklist" for developing countries, presented at disaster relief seminar in Geneva in October.

1984   June 1: in his sixtieth year, resigned as president of Food for the Hungry International, to be succeeded by Dr. Tetsunao Yamamori—completing the full internationalization of the FHI program as he had long anticipated.

This is the bare bones outline. The flesh-and-blood substance: the countless thousands of lives he has touched around the world. The heart of all the above: "This poor man cried, and the Lord heard him. . . ."

four
"FACT, FAITH, FEELING..."

To Larry Ward, God himself is the fundamental fact of the universe. Larry is fond of quoting "fact, faith, feeling" as the divine order for—well, just about everything.

"Our eternal salvation is based upon the fact of God himself," Larry maintains. *"He* exists, *he* loves, *he* gave his Son to die in our place. *He* calls us to himself—and *he* gives us the faith to respond.

"If someone tells me he has sincerely trusted Christ to be his Savior, in obedience to the Word of God, but somehow doesn't 'feel' saved, I tell him not to worry about it. The 'feeling' will come, as the Holy Spirit works in his life and as he grows spiritually. But we start with the *fact* of a loving God who invites us to come to him, and promises that he will not 'cast us out' when we do."

Similarly, with reference to his work for the hungry, Larry tells people that even though they may not have seen the world of hunger as he has seen it, and may not "feel" its heartbreak as he feels it (because they haven't seen it firsthand, or perhaps because their emotional makeup is not the same as his), this is no excuse for not getting helpfully involved. "Again," he says, "we start with the fact of God. *He* cares about the hungry. We know he does, because there is more than abundant evidence of this in his Word. And he has specifically mandated us to do something about it. We find that over and over again, in the Bible."

"HOLY BIBLE, BOOK DIVINE . . ."

Larry Ward doesn't seem to care much about "things."

Cars, clothing, material possessions in general—these don't "turn him on," *unless* they somehow relate to helping other people.

But there is one thing Larry does treasure: his Bible.

"Larry doesn't hold his Bible, he caresses it," someone observed.

While Larry Ward himself would warn against "bibliolatry" (worship of the Word instead of the God for whom it speaks), he admits to a constant feeling of "reverential awe" when he handles and reads the Bible.

Lorraine has noticed that Larry never puts anything (such as another book) on top of his Bible. If someone else does, he quickly moves it.

I once saw him with tears in his eyes as he stood behind a church pulpit and addressed himself to the book in his hand (quoting an old hymn): "Holy Bible, book divine—precious treasure, thou art *mine!*"

No doubt many people have contributed to this attitude. Larry himself would cite his father ("He fell in love with the Bible almost the moment he became a Christian") and his godly preacher father-in-law Rev. L. P. Hustad ("a big 'man's man' who would weep as he preached, just from the sheer joy of being privileged to communicate the truth of God"). He points to the example of faithful preacher-friends such as R. T. Ketcham and A. W. Tozer, and the biblically oriented ministries of former pastors such as Reginald Matthews, John Anderson, Bernard Travaille, and Guy Davidson. In Wheaton College's 1946 fall evangelistic series (Larry's first year back after military service), Dr. Merv Rosell had a marked impression on Larry's life. The two have remained close friends. Larry is fond of describing Merv with Cliff Barrows' phrase, "The Apostle of Encouragement."

No matter where he is or how early the hour, Larry's first appointment each day is with God—with the Bible (usually a chapter each day) and his *Living Light* daily reading.

"THE WAY, THE *TRUTH . . ."*

Larry's love for God's truth carries over into a firm stand for truth and honesty in every area of life.

"My dear mom," he recalls with a chuckle, "knew how to stop me in my tracks if I started to come up with a little boy whopper. She would just look into my eyes and ask, 'Honest?' That may not have been very grammatical, but it was very effective. No way could I lie to her! I would just sorta melt and say something like, 'No, Mom. It wasn't a tiger, it was just a big ole cat. Well, not such a big one, I guess. And he didn't really chase me; he just looked at me kinda mean like. . . .'"

And this preoccupation with truth has been intensified through Larry's editorial background. To him, words are almost sacred. They are a gift of God, made for full and honest communication.

"I try to be an appreciative listener in church," says Larry. "I have to give out so much that I am always grateful when I can take in. But I admit it really bothers me when I hear some preacher tell a more-than-twice-told-tale as his own, or bend a story or adapt a punchline so it neatly fits his own sermon outline."

And perhaps this is why he regards gossip as such a serious sin. "I knew a preacher once whose ministry was almost ruined by careless talk. Later it was found that none of it was true."

And it has come even closer than that to Larry Ward. One of his colleagues suffered a painful marriage breakup and subsequently remarried. Larry spent many months (and hundreds of hours) in a counseling role, along with a professional counselor. He was acquainted with every detail of the situation. It was painful for him, for he loved both the people involved. But the greatest pain came when people not that close to the situation began to pick it up and "broadcast" it to the world—without a full appreciation of the facts.

Larry shakes his head as he recalls: "One particular 'Christian leader'—who had no firsthand contact with the situation—was quoted to me by people in various parts of the country (and of the world, for that matter) as having brought this up to them and being very critical of my colleague. But when I confronted him (honestly wondering if he might somehow have information I myself had missed), he denied even having made those statements which other people were independently attributing to him. Very strange! And then an organization which had given us some money told us it had been strongly criticized by a 'Christian leader' for doing so because of this same situation—and once again the same inaccurate statements had been made. I guess it's true, sadly true, that a lie can go around the world while truth is still on the launching pad."

The significant thing about this instance is that Larry was not just being loyal to an old friend. He was standing for the truth, as he saw it.

Larry's Civil War novel, *Thy Brother's Blood,* is of course fictional, but it seems to reflect his own philosophy. In the last chapter Wade Andrews confronts his brother Stephen. They had served on opposite sides in the war; they had even fought (at the insistence of Stephen, the Christian brother) when they met during the battle of Front Royal, Virginia. Now Wade had become a Christian, partly through the witness of General Stonewall Jackson, the great Christian leader of the Confederacy. But the major influence, Wade testifies, had been the example of Stephen, "a man to whom truth was truth so much that he would pick up a gun he hated, and kill men he loved—and even fight with his own brother."

One has the feeling that—in that paragraph, at least—

Larry was being autobiographical. That's the kind of value he himself places upon truth.

THE CHURCH HIS BODY

Another concept very important to Larry Ward is that of the Church (all true believers in Christ around the world) as the mystical "body" of Christ.

To be sure, Larry (probably because of his Baptist background) is very much a local church enthusiast. He believes in "the church on the corner as well as the church in the world."

But he does feel a special and very strong commitment to that "body" of believers all around the world. And this is reflected even in the basic organization of Food for the Hungry.

During our days together at World Vision I often heard Larry sketch his view of the ideal organizational pattern for any worldwide mission type organization: a truly international staff; operating from a neutral base (such as Geneva, Switzerland) with "support entities" in those countries which could supply both funding and human resources. He deeply appreciated World Vision's commitment to effective internationalization and was an active member of their committee designed to bring it about.

When Food for the Hungry was formed in 1971, this was his chance to build "from the ground up" another agency with true international character. Today it exists—an international coordinating center in Geneva . . . a network of ten service offices scattered throughout the world in places of desperate need . . . a truly international staff, with some eight different nationalities, director-level and up . . . and support entities in the United States, Australia, and Japan—with more "on the drawing board."

The entity in Japan is of particular interest to Larry. He tells about his involvements with Bob Pierce in the Osaka and Tokyo crusades in 1959 and 1961, and is very grateful to Bob for the concept of organizations as "the servant of the church" around the world. He is deeply grateful to friends such as missionary Joe Gooden in Japan for reinforcing that understanding.

It was during the Osaka crusade in 1959 that Larry actually put down in specifics the organizational concepts which were to find eventual and specific reality in Food for the Hungry. It was a source of great satisfaction to him, therefore, in 1983 to sit in Osaka with a founding group of Japanese Christians as they organized "Food for the Hungry/Japan."

The concept is not that of Japan's being a recipient country—one being helped—but rather one supplying "food and funds and friends" to the rest of the world.

Larry says: "I have marveled at the way Japanese ingenuity, technology, and managerial genius have impacted the world. I have coveted that same influence on behalf of the work of God in the world, and specifically for the hungry."

LOOKING AHEAD . . .

And it was probably a commitment to all of these things— truth, honesty, and the worldwide family of God—which led Larry to a very important decision in about 1981.

He has always been very candid about his role in Food for the Hungry. "I didn't have to be the head of anything," he says. "There was just a job to be done; I saw no one else doing it with an organization specifically designed to help the hungry as its prime objective, really 'the only string on its guitar,' and so with a group of concerned friends I launched Food for the Hungry."

Larry was keenly aware of a pattern he had seen very often in Christian work. He has served on many boards, and has been in close touch with a great variety of Christian organizations.

He had often seen an organization begin, as it had to,

with what someone has termed "an entrepreneurial generalist, or a generalist entrepreneur"—and in time outgrow its founder.

Larry chuckles as he describes this sort of scenario. "The day comes when the organization has outgrown its founder. The specialists have arrived—and now that generalist-founder is the bottleneck. So everyone wonders what to do. They shake their heads, look over at the founder in the corner and whisper something like, 'Poor ole Larry. How are we going to tell him? It will break his heart.'"

Whether or not Food for the Hungry was at that point or even beginning to approach it didn't matter. Larry's commitment to the hungry was such that he was willing to step aside for the good of the organization.

He startled his board therefore in July 1981, with the bold recommendation that one of his chief colleagues—Japanese-born Dr. Tetsunao Yamamori—be named President-Elect.

He proposed at least a two-year transition period, to assist Dr. Yamamori in taking over the complex aspects of both the international program and the support aspects . . . and also to acquaint both government leadership worldwide and the support constituencies (in the United States, primarily) with Dr. Yamamori.

"Ted Yamamori has a deep devotion to Christ, a strong and effective leadership style—and a managerial genius. Food for the Hungry has arrived at a place where it needs this kind of leadership, and I know that Dr. Yamamori will take the organization far beyond any heights that it could ever reach under my leadership alone."

Larry Ward and Tetsunao Yamamori are very different personalities. But they have developed a close bond of fellowship in helping the hungry, with a very effective working relationship based on their strong mutual respect.

Larry has agreed to serve for a time as board chairman, after Dr. Yamamori assumes the presidency of Food for the Hungry in 1984.

He is particularly happy about Dr. Yamamori's experience, as a disciple of Dr. Donald McGavran, in the field of church growth. To Larry, the way to do relief and development so they actually result in evangelism and in the growth of the church around the world is to be strongly related to the national churches—to work in effective partnership with them.

That's Tetsunao Yamamori's conviction and working pattern, and that is one of the reasons why "I thank God for him so very much."

Larry sees Dr. Yamamori as a strong "team leader"—and knows he will be ably assisted by Vice President Bill Moy in the U.S., and by Vice Presidents Homer Dowdy, Dulal Borpujari, and John Fitzstevens on the international side.

What's ahead for Larry Ward, as he steps aside from the active presidency of Food for the Hungry International? "I don't know, exactly," Larry says, "but I am very much at peace. I do want to keep on being 'a voice to plead the cause of the poor and needy,' and I expect to be much more involved in speaking ministries throughout the United States and in Canada—and around the world. I have all sorts of notes tucked away here and there as the bases for articles and books I want to write. So we will just see how God leads, step by step."

One thing is certain. Larry meant it when he said it back there on the shores of Canandaigua Lake at Le Tourneau Christian Camp in 1940: "Where he leads me, I will follow."

Just how deep is Larry Ward's commitment to truth and "rightness"? There's a rather clear indication in a signed and notarized statement he issued in August, 1981. It was officially witnessed by Lorraine, on behalf of the family, and by Tetsunao Yamamori, representing Food for the Hungry.

Larry had been deeply concerned about the rise of international terrorism and the spectacle of Americans abroad being held for ransom. His statement directed that in the event of his being kidnapped or held hostage "no negotiations of any kind are to be conducted with terrorist groups."

Household name he isn't, but Larry is constantly in the world's hot spots. He has been a dinner guest in presidential palaces in such areas as Bangladesh, Vietnam, Nicaragua, and Guatemala. He has had official meetings with controversial leaders such as Nicaragua's Somoza and Bangladesh's Sheik Mujib—both of whom were later assassinated. He has escaped coups and near-coups in Thailand and Bolivia, and has been with some of Lebanon's top leaders in the midst of their shooting war.

Aware that, humanly speaking, he just "might be in the right place at the wrong time" and be captured, Larry stated: "It is my specific desire that not one cent of money or moment of time be expended in any negotiations for my release."

He summed it up: "I fully support the present strong position taken against terrorism by the U.S. government. International gangsterism must be stopped. As a relief worker, I am totally expendable. As a Christian, I gladly put myself in the hand of our all-powerful God."

Larry suggested that if he is kidnapped or held hostage, his notarized letter should simply be published with this notation for captors: "He's all yours. You can have him."

five

A LOVE LETTER TO A FLAG
by Larry Ward

These 650 words, used by permission from the Montrose, California, *Ledger* newspaper which published them in 1974, offer a glimpse of Larry Ward's deep-seated love of country.

Let's face it—I'm a square. An unabashed, unashamed ready-to-stand-up-and-be-counted square.

I mean, who else but a square would write a love letter to a flag?

It was December 1941, and Old Glory was waving there in the winter winds of Upstate New York. Nobody had had to suggest it; it wasn't a planned thing—but there we were by the dozens that Monday morning, that strange morning after, that Pearl Harbor Monday of December 8.

And I was there, sixteen and unhesitatingly ready to lie about my age like every other underage kid in town. I can still see that grizzled recruiting sergeant, shaking his head and barking: "All right, all you guys that ain't old enough. It won't do you no good. We hafta check. So go home."

But I noted he spoke with a sort of gruff tenderness and warmth, and I felt that his voice quivered a bit as he added, "—but thank you!"—and then turned quickly away.

And you were there, Old Stars and Stripes, Old Glory. I don't think I had ever really seen you before — waving proud and somehow defiant over the Norwich Courthouse. And my heart saluted you before I walked away.

An ambassador from another country said it to me once, as we discussed his country's controversial new flag: "I suppose," he said thoughtfully, "a country doesn't really appreciate its flag until it has fought a war under it." Well, by that criterion, we should appreciate you, our flag!

I remember another year and another war, a strange and different war. I was there in Saigon on that awful day in 1965 when a vicious explosion ripped through the siesta quiet.

I raced through the streets to a scene of carnage and horror. A bomb had been exploded outside the American Embassy. I saw the shattered building and the broken bodies of the dead and dying; I knelt beside the young American Marine guard and vainly sought his pulse. And then I lifted my eyes and saw you, Ole American Flag, hanging there limp and torn. And that gaping hole which had ripped your stripes somehow symbolized the emptiness in the heart of our country, the gash which the Vietnam controversy tore open there.

Of course I have seen you in happier days, Beloved Flag! You have welcomed me home those 200-plus times when I've come back from other shores . . . you have stirred my heart when I have seen you in Moscow and Phnom Penh and Berlin and around the globe . . . and you have especially caused my heart to throw that old and respectful salute when I have just come back from the refugee camps of earth — after I have walked among those who have fled before the cruel face of oppression.

For me you always float in freedom when I see you at full mast . . . and the sneer on the face of the pseudo-sophisticate as he reads these words doesn't bother me one bit! If he had walked where I have walked and heard what I have heard, if his hands had been stained (as mine so tragically often have been) with the blood of those who died for freedom, their own or someone else's—perhaps he'd have the guts and the gratitude to join me as I stand and salute you once more.

Flag, you hang over special heartache today. We have to strain to see you through the pollution of corruption and confusion. But you're still there, and we see you! And if I don't have a hat when you go by, I'll borrow one just so I can take it off in deep respect!

I don't know if anyone ever wrote a love letter to a flag before.

I don't care, really. This is mine. And so my heart salutes again . . . in respect, in gratitude, and yes—in love.

six

SACRED JOYS OF HOME

Notable persons usually enter this world incognito. Ralph Waldo Emerson liked to put his hand reverently upon the head of any urchin, thinking he "may be patting the head of a future president."

On December 14, 1924, in Sidney, New York, Max, June, Whitney, and Doris patted the head of their wee brother to whom their parents gave the name of Lawrence Edward.

A. W. Tozer pointed out that if you get a good mother it will not do to be too particular about your father; "you cannot have both." This tiny boy seemed to have had both, however. From thin, wiry, gregarious, artistic Whitney Ward, Larry inherited a fondness for people; his chunky little mother, Orleva, gave him a rugged physical constitution, a warm and optimistic spirit, and a calm disposition which leaves him unflappable in the most unnerving of situations.

A person passing by the Ward house in Upstate New York during the Roaring Twenties might have seen Whitney tap dancing for his children as he had done with the Hi Henry Minstrels, or juggling Orleva's best china, or entertaining them with his ventriloquist dummy perched on his knee.

A passerby during the Christmas season of 1926 would have seen something quite different: Orleva hurrying with cold packs to cool the fevered brow of her youngest. . . . Whitney sitting beside the crib watching pneumonia attempt to steal the life of his son. When doctors could do no more, Whitney stood awkwardly beside the crib and lifted his eyes. Strange recollections of forgotten convictions stirred within. "God," he whispered, "if you'll heal my son, he's yours."

Before the sun rose, Larry began to recover. The encounter had driven a stake for righteousness into the soul of Whitney Ward that God would later claim, partly through the witness of that youngest Ward for whom the father had prayed.

When economic reverses touched the artist, he moved his brood into his mother's big brick house in Cooperstown, New York. Grandma's house was a suitable base for flights of fancy as the children roamed from attic to basement to the barn out back, seldom finding the cookie jar on the cellar steps empty.

High on a hayloft one day, Larry called out, "Watch me fly!" The preschooler leaped and flew—straight to the barn floor, bruised but unbroken. On another day during a game on the barn floor, he tagged a door which flew open, propelling him out into the trackless air above the barnyard. His brothers and sisters rushed down the stairs expecting to see him torn and bleeding, maybe dead. The only "injury" was the absence of breath which dramatic gasping and some crying quickly restored.

"The spankings we four older kids received for 'not watching Larry' hurt us more than his bruises hurt him," recalls sister June as she remembered the day Larry rode his tricycle down a flight of stairs with a paring knife in his hand.

The world of 1928 was small for the youngest Ward. He knew little beyond the appointed rounds of his tricycle and the warm protection of Grandma Hine's lap where he learned to read. As a boy of four he caught on to sight reading, not just words, but whole sentences and eventually paragraphs. The earliest book he remembers reading is the classic *Ivanhoe,* Sir Walter Scott's recounting of the return of King Richard the Lionhearted from captivity. Grandma Hine's early training helped him eventually to read virtually by pages rather than word by word. Before he had finished elementary school Larry could read 930 words per minute with almost total comprehension. This ability would later give him an edge in editorial endeavors.

After a love of books came a passion for sports, neither of which has diminished. Note the day when he transferred to East Main Street Elementary School in Norwich and ran through virtually the entire school in a football scrimmage, reaching the goal line with his necktie torn off and his shirt shredded. Note the day when he gratefully accepted a pair of boxing gloves to fight in the selected fraternity of pint-sized sportsmen at East Main School by knocking down Clif Frink with one punch, a kid so agile he later became an AAU boxer. To Larry it was all fun. "I wasn't mad at anybody," he told his mother.

As a seventh grader in Norwich Junior High he hit four home runs in five times at bat in a softball game—the first in the district's newly organized 1936 sports program. *The Norwich Evening Sun* headlined his achievement: "Ward Hits Four Homers."

On Halloween night that year, eleven-year-old Larry Ward wound up in the jailhouse with his friend Dave Miller after a raid on a cabbage patch. The boys thought a pile of cabbages would look good stacked on the school principal's porch. Police interrupted the raid and hauled the boys in for questioning. One by one the officers lectured the repentant, tearful pranksters and released them when they promised never to do it again.

Before the Norwich Municipal Pool was built, swimming required a hike up to the railroad bridge north of town. Larry and his friends would swing out on a rope, Tarzan style, to plunge into the creek. Sometimes they would stand on the track as the Delaware and Lackawana engine approached and jump only at the last possible moment, the train's horn blaring and its brakes hissing.

In the late weeks of 1934's winter, when the wooded hills of Norwich showed signs of spring, the Ward family all were headed for a mighty turning. Larry's classmate, Levi Brooker, invited him to tag along one afternoon at two-thirty to a "released time" class at Calvary Baptist Church.

"It's not like school," Levi explained. "It's fun."

The idea of church was not appealing, but an early afternoon release from school was too good to pass up. Larry persuaded his sisters June and Doris and brother Whitney to go with him to the Regular Baptist Church on Birdsall Street. Evangelist Adam Lutzweiler was ready. The versatile visiting minister entertained the children with his marimba and told them a simple story from the Bible. He pressed upon them the claims of Jesus Christ and invited them to say yes to the Savior's call.

Whitney and Orleva were amazed by what they heard coming out of the mouths of their babies. Somewhere in the past the father had faced these claims and turned away. Orleva had been a Methodist but had followed afar off because of her husband's lack of interest.

Now on Easter Sunday, 1934, they found themselves seated in Calvary Baptist Church watching as four of their children were being baptized. The youthful testimonies were heard; and then the children were lowered into the baptismal waters where they were identified with Christ in his death, burial, and resurrection.

Pastor Norman MacPherson delivered a short message that evening. He finished by inviting sinners in the audience to make their peace with God. Whitney Earl Ward was the first one in the aisle. He practically ran to the altar with Orleva right behind him. What an Easter celebration with hugs, warm words of praise to God, resolutions, and deep-down joy.

Larry had a different father from that night on. Whitney fell instanty in love with the Scriptures. It was not unusual for Larry to come home after midnight from a wrestling match to find his father at the kitchen table poring over the Bible with *Bancroft's Systematic Theology* at his side. He itinerated as a lay preacher throughout the area, gave his testimony at every opportunity, painted Scripture verses on his car, and preached on street corners.

In gratitude to Calvary Baptist Church for his regeneration, he painted a life-size portrait of Christ over the baptistry. Whitney joined The Gideons and helped to distribute copies of the Bible throughout Upstate New York. God had remembered Whitney's prayer beside the "dying bed" of his baby son and had responded by bringing light and life and salvation to all of his house.

seven
GOALS TO GO

Larry was thirteen in 1938 when he lined up with incoming freshmen at Norwich High. Four years later when he stood with his class he was graduated with high honors, had earned the coveted George McMullen Award "for doing the most for his school," and had distinguished himself as the winner of more awards and honors than anyone else to that date at Norwich High.

School chum David Miller remembers Larry as "always the center of attention at school. He was liked by girls, boys, and teachers alike. He seldom took a book home to study, but managed to earn the top grades. Larry won letters in football, wrestling, and track. He was active also in various organizations and was often the president of groups ranging from the Chi Alpha Honor Society to the Boys' Athletic Council."

With David, Larry hitchhiked to football games in the Ivy League circuit, attended the popular Boys' State forum in Syracuse, and knew no higher goal than to please Coach Kurt Beyer at Norwich High.

"When the various teams would travel to out-of-town events," David recalls, "everyone wanted to be in the same car as Larry. He was an endless reservoir of humorous stories and puns. One time only the best players on our football team went to a game on Long Island. Larry went, but on his return he noted my crestfallen state because I had not been chosen.

"'Aw, you didn't miss anything,' he told me. 'I'm sorry I went.' He proceeded to tell me that the team lost, that he was sick on the bus, and that the entire trip was one I should be happy indeed to have missed—all this just to make me feel better. He was compassionate even then."

The trait of fighting for the underdog emerged in high school. In front of Larry in one of his classes sat a mild little Church of the Nazarene kid, shy Howard Newton. "The teacher that year was probably an alcoholic," Larry says, recalling the experiences. "She would drag into class each morning with an enormous hangover. Nobody in the class knew what was wrong with her."

She asked Howard a question one morning which he misunderstood. The teacher angrily scolded him with bitter words and made him a spectacle. Larry jumped to his feet. "That's it!" he shouted. "I've had it!"

Wow, he thought, *what do I do now?*

The teacher leveled a finger at him. "You're a Communist!" she shouted back. "You're a Communist agitator and you're up to no good. Go to the principal's office immediately."

Trembling as he walked out of the room, Larry glumly made his way to the office of Russell L. Hogue. Teachers had always been his friends. So had the principal. Now he had blown it.

"I just felt sorry for Howie Newton," Larry explained. "He is innocent and I couldn't help myself."

"Well, Larry," the principal replied, "your teacher has a problem. We all know about it. Probably it would be best to have you switch classes."

Coach Kurt Beyer, who later earned a place in the National Interscholastic Hall of Fame, became an idol to the youngest Ward at Norwich High. "Coach" could coax from his boys heroic efforts on the playing fields. When Stanford University made the T-formation famous, Coach Beyer was the first in New York to bring it into high school football, and Larry Ward was one of the first T-formation quarterbacks. Coach Beyer drilled his teams in the fundamentals. He was clever enough to know the limitations and the strong points of each team.

In 1937, Leo Bolley from Syracuse came on the radio to announce his selections for the all-state football team.

"This year my job is easy," Bolley began. One by one he named the players of the undefeated and unscored-on Norwich High School team.

At the height of his football career as a high school sophomore, Larry broke his right leg in a game. As a senior he broke the left one. For weeks he hobbled on his appointed campus rounds with crutches—his brothers and sisters proud of their little brother who had "given his all" for dear old Norwich High.

Larry wanted badly to play basketball, but at five feet, six inches tall, his chances were modified. Wrestling offered a new challenge of individual strength and skill; and since "Coach" needed another man on the wrestling team, that would be it.

The evening of Larry's first match took him to Van Hornesville High School. His opponent had hair all over his chest and the skill and strength expected to go with it. In a few seconds Larry was pinned. Humiliated, he shook hands and headed for the shower. Basketball looked more and more appealing. But the more he thought about wrestling, the more he was challenged by it. He would stick around until he won some matches, to erase the memory of this first embarrassing defeat. Besides, if that's what Coach wanted. . . .

Endless exercises for his neck muscles pushed his shirt size up . . . up . . . up. His already broad shoulders grew thick and his grip became like iron. In one of his last high school wrestling matches, he went back to Van Hornesville and wrestled the brother of the guy who had pinned him at the start. Larry had him in thirty seconds.

"Wrestling teaches independence," he says. "In football you could miss a catch or fumble the ball and the team would still be there. But in wrestling it's you out there alone against your opponent, and that teaches a special kind of personal responsibility."

Will Rogers said he never met a man he didn't like. Larry could probably say that too, but he could also say quite confidently, "I've never met a man I couldn't lick." Gentle by nature though he is, that quiet confidence has carried him through many difficult and dangerous situations, especially in the battlefields and disaster areas where his work has taken him.

Larry wrote the senior class' motto at Norwich: "He profits most who serves best." He also wrote the class poem which showed his knowledge of a world beyond the confines of Upstate New York, a world then plunged into global war, a world in need which could offer a place for him to serve:

A world of turmoil,
A world of strife,
We see as we stand
On the threshold of life . . .
But we face a bright tomorrow.

All history has been
A record of war.
We look to the future,
Expecting more . . .
Yet we face a bright tomorrow.

Our future is bright because
We carry light and truth
and liberty
To a world of darkness.

His passion for sports directed his goal toward a career in coaching until that memorable night of July 11, 1940. As a staff worker at LeTourneau Camp on Lake Canandaigua, New York, he was in the tabernacle that summer night when Ralph W. Neighbor got up to preach. His delivery was unpretentious, his message now forgotten. But the urgency of his appeal became the voice of God to staffer Larry Ward.

As the youthful audience sang softly, "Where he leads me I will follow," Larry decided, "That's for me." He walked forward, stood in sawdust at the rustic altar, and tearfully gave to the Lord the reins of his heart. At the age of fifteen Larry was licensed to preach by Calvary Baptist Church of Norwich.

eight
INTO THE BRAZEN THROAT OF WAR

The winds of war were blowing briskly that spring day of 1942 when Larry was called into the office of Principal Russell L. Hogue at Norwich High. Graduation was a few weeks away. Selected members of the faculty had gathered and Larry was asked to take a seat.

"Well!" Principal Hogue exclaimed, rubbing his hands together. "Larry, we have some good news for you today."

The faculty members beamed.

Mr. Hogue picked up a sheaf of papers, tapped them on his desk to make them even, then handed them to his star pupil. "We have here a full scholarship to Duke University in Durham, North Carolina, for Lawrence Edward Ward."

"There's a theology school there, too," added Guidance Director Marcia Stewart enthusiastically, knowing of Larry's Christian commitment. "You could go right into that, with full tuition, after you finish university."

Larry hesitated. He could read on their faces what his response should have been.

"Thanks," he said, promising to read the material carefully.

He had noticed earlier an obscure news item on the sports page of the *Binghamton Sun* that the wrestling team of Wheaton College in Illinois had prayed before getting out on the mat. *A winning wrestling team that prayed together! What a privilege it would be to attend that school!* he thought.

"I appreciate the scholarship," Larry told Dr. Hogue the next day, looking past him to the Wheaton College catalog on the shelf. "But . . . I was thinking . . . maybe Wheaton would be the place where I'd like to. . . ."

Dr. Hogue frowned. "Yes, well. . . . " He wheeled around and pulled the catalog off the shelf. "Sort of a Bible school, isn't it?"

He leafed through the pages, frowning. "Well, if that's what you want, I'll check it out."

Unrelated letters from the principal, from Dr. Harold Strathearn at LeTourneau Evangelistic Center in New York, and from his pastor to Wheaton's President, V. Raymond Edman, resulted in a scholarship at a school distinguished as a training ground for the world's top Christian leaders. (Billy Graham was a senior when Larry enrolled as a freshman on September 12, 1942.)

Later schoolmates at Wheaton included three who became missionaries to Ecuador and were murdered by fierce Auca Indians—Jim Elliot, Ed McCully, and Nate Saint.

In front of Pierce Chapel hung a large flag on which a gold star appeared each time a Wheaton man was killed on the battlefields of World War II. A war-conscious campus monitored the troop movements abroad and prayed for the far-flung fighting alumni of the eighty-two-year-old school.

The semester ground on and the war theaters grew hotter. A united nation prayed for peace but continued to prepare for the bloodiest encounters against the Japanese expansionists and Hitler with his wild dreams of world conquest.

On December 7, 1942, all campus activities paused to mark World War II's first anniversary. Strong men began disappearing from class to join the allied forces. The voice of President Franklin Delano Roosevelt assured the youth of the nation that there was a place for them on the front lines, where thunder to thunder spoke. The nightly radio news brought grim reports from the South Pacific and the European bases where the artificial plague of man ground on.

On December 14, Larry was eighteen—old enough to enlist. One month later, at the end of the first semester at Wheaton, he reported for duty in the United States Air Force (then the Army Air Corps). He was assigned the number 32837111. In his farewell to college joys, "this poor man cried" to God, asking for directions in this new life.

Early in his army career he received an unexpected pass which would enable him to travel home. "Here's my chance to surprise everyone," he decided.

Arriving at the Norwich Greyhound bus station, he walked a few blocks to his house. Peeking through the front window, he saw his mother sitting in the living room reading. Deciding to play it cool, Larry opened the door and strolled in. "Hi," he said casually.

Orleva, equal to the occasion, calmly replied, "Hi," and then returned to her reading.

Larry stood there awkwardly, a bit crushed and not knowing what to do next. And then he saw the little smile playing at the corner of her mouth.

"Did you wipe your feet?" his mother asked.

Then came the cries of joy, the hugs, the tears, and the long visits to catch up on the news before Uncle Sam beckoned and it was time to return to war.

Although Larry volunteered to join a squadron heading for Germany, his assignments in the military kept him in the United States and its Alaskan territory. After instruction as an aerial gunner in Nevada, he was sent to Florida for training which led to a position, at age nineteen, as instructor for new recruits. From there he was sent to Ladd Field at Fairbanks, Alaska, and finally to a detachment in Watertown, South Dakota.

In Alaska, days were short and nights were long for most of this mission. A bright spot was an abandoned library on the base. After a day of flying, even before he shed his flight suit, he would slip into the library and read. He remembers reading all of the fiction of Grace Livingston Hill and other books available to a lonely gunner in a remote war.

In Watertown, South Dakota, a memorable morning stands out in his recollections. His unit was assigned to a training flight to practice air-to-ground firing. The men were instructed to try to bring the target down by firing at the base of a certain structure.

"But remember," the dispatcher intoned, "fire only off the *left* side of the plane. There'll be an abandoned red barn and a white house near the windmill."

Larry suited up and crawled into the plexiglass-covered tail of a B-25 bomber. Soon he was roaring down the runway and lifting off into the blue for the firing practice run. Its altitude reached, the twin-engine plane banked and started down. Larry looked to the left. Sure enough, there was the abandoned farm house and the red barn and the windmill which they were to knock down.

Rat-a-tat-a-tat. . . . His tracers were finding their mark beautifully. Funny thing, though, he noted that there were chickens running around down there. Chickens at an abandoned farm house? Oh, well. . . . He kept firing.

Just as he took aim on the second pass, he felt someone pulling his leg. His first impulse was to keep firing and check later on what his buddy wanted.

The airman was pale. "S-stop!" he gasped. "We've got the wrong windmill!"

The farmer and his wife had dived under the bed at the first pass, but had managed to call the operations office only after three more attacks to stop their friendly enemy from pouring more lead into their "abandoned" farm.

With the maturing that came from his military service, Larry sensed the need for someone to share his life—someone with the same dedication and willingness to follow the ways of God. In Watertown he enjoyed the unusual experience of serving as the founding director of what became a thriving Youth For Christ rally program. He selected for his own place of worship the Christian and Missionary Alliance Church. A small decision, perhaps, but broad in its implications, for in that small congregation Larry found the sweetest person in his life—who was also gentle, patient, and well suited to support him in his God-ordained career.

nine
A HOME AND A CAREER

A week of special evangelistic services was planned at the Watertown Christian and Missionary Alliance Church. One evening Larry returned to town after roaming the skies in a bomber over the Black Hills. He hurried into church and slipped into a back pew to enjoy the service.

He noticed with sudden interest the guest pianist whose back was toward the congregation. When the song ended and she turned around, his eyes widened and his heart stopped. Before him was the most beautiful girl he had ever seen. There followed the longest sermon he had ever heard, for his eyes were not on Evangelist Vance Berg, but on the back of the head of visiting Lorraine Hustad from Hibbing, Minnesota, the daughter of the former pastor in Watertown.

At the sound of the Amen, Larry zigzagged through the pews to the opposite side of the sanctuary and blurted out, "Hi, I'm Larry Ward."

Oh, no, Lorraine groaned inwardly, *not one of those obnoxious flyers at the air base.*

The soldiers, in the opinion of the Watertowners, had ruined their city. *At least he's in church,* she concluded as she looked him over.

Lorraine had received her nurses' training at Luther

Hospital in Watertown, so she was altogether familiar with the Air Base. When her parents moved to Hibbing on the famed Mesabi Iron Range, she moved there and found a position in a hospital, but had returned now to visit some friends.

Larry worked fast. He attended church every night that week. To a mutual friend, Mrs. Ila White, he confided one night, "I think she's terrific!"

"Well, you know, don't you?" Mrs. White whispered. "She's leaving tomorrow for Echo, Minnesota."

Larry quickly obtained a three-day pass, bought a ticket to Echo on the Minnesota and St. Louis Line, and boarded at the Watertown Station. As he walked through the train looking for Lorraine, he found her seated near the back of an empty car—the only passenger on the train. As he stepped in he hurried to her side and asked, "Is this seat taken?"

The conductor punched his ticket, winked, left, and never returned during the entire trip except once to report that the engineer was stopping the train to shoot a pheasant.

On the two-hour journey the new friends spoke of many things—themselves, the Christian and Missionary Alliance, the war and finally . . . Grandma Hustad, whom he would meet at the end of the line in Echo.

Larry already knew other members of the Hustad family: Lorraine's parents, her pastor-cousin David, and another cousin, famed Christian organist and composer-arranger Donald P. Hustad.

"By the time the train stopped I was hopelessly hooked," he said. "I was ready to meet the matriarchal Grandma Hustad or anyone else who might have stood in my way."

Lorraine introduced her new friend and Grandma looked him over. "He's just a friend from Watertown," Lorraine explained.

"She says he's just a friend," Grandma reported to the family, "but I think there's more to it than that."

Selecting a girl from such a beautiful family was to Larry a "wonderful bonus." He wanted no casual affair. After that train ride they were off and running. Under his pillow at the base went an encouraging letter from Lorraine and the photograph that was enclosed.

The date of July 5, 1947, was already affixed in the time table of God's providence. After a year at Wheaton College, Larry took his campus (and military) buddy Bob "Old Sarge" Baker to Hibbing and proudly stood at the altar to receive his bride. He had never proposed and run the risk of receiving a negative reply. But the actions of a man are the best interpreters of his thoughts, so Lorraine had little doubted his intentions all along.

Lorraine Alice Hustad Ward had made her commitment to Jesus Christ at the age of eight years. An only child, she was reared in a quiet home free of tension or disunion. Her supportive attitude toward the ministry of Christ, her ability to endure her husband's long absences as he has traveled the world in missionary endeavors, her thrift, serenity, and home management have made her the perfect mate for her peripatetic man.

"What does a wife do when her husband follows the kind of work that keeps him away from home?" Lorraine reflected on their thirty-fifth wedding anniversary. "Some marriages survive, some don't. A wife must feel a part of the ministry. This kind of love requires a bit of courage and a bit of wisdom in handling the children."

A year and a half before his marriage, Larry had been mustered out of the service on January 29, 1946. He had returned to civilian life with a fiancée, a modest savings account, and hours of experience both in the work of war and of preaching the gospel. Since it was too late to enroll for Wheaton's spring semester, he had answered an urgent plea for help from an old friend and joined the staff of the LeTourneau Evangelistic Center in New York City. One of his assignments had been editing *The Joyful News*. There his appetite for Christian journalism was sharpened, and during that period he sold his first published piece.

It was a tract titled, "Believing and Behaving," the subject for which arose out of a series of experiences in New York City. While he was getting a haircut on Eighth Avenue one day, the barber remarked, "Your hair's getting thin. You ought to try our special tonic. No use losing your hair, young fellow."

Larry was impressed—until he looked up and noticed that the barber was as bald as a cue ball.

A little later on the street a newsboy called, "Extra! Extra! Read all about it! Paper, Mister?"

"Well, what's the news?" Larry asked.

"How should I know?" the boy replied. "I never read the paper."

Larry stored away in his memory those two amusing experiences. They clicked because they occurred so closely together. Then, to make the series complete, he encountered a third on the next day. As he was studying a menu in the New York restaurant called "A Bird in the Hand," he asked the waitress what she recommended.

"Couldn't tell you," she replied. "I never eat here."

Larry remembered the story of the old preacher who told his congregation: "There are two things every Christian has to do. We have to believe the gospel—and behave the gospel."

The barber was talking about what his hair tonic would do but he wasn't applying it. The newsboy was urging others to read the news when he didn't know what it was. The waitress was serving nourishing food to others which she had never tried.

Larry's tract, "Believing and Behaving," was published in 1946, "full of all the clichés and corny expressions you can think of," according to the author, "but it must have had a message for the heart, because it went through several printings. A missionary in Africa found it in his Bible a few months ago, and here and there I've heard preachers give those same illustrations in sermons."

In September 1946, Larry had returned to his studies in

Wheaton. He had heard that Robert Walker, editor of *His* magazine and of *Sunday Magazine* (which later merged with *Christian Life and Times* to become *Christian Life)*, was teaching at Wheaton. Larry took all the classes he could from Walker and became satisfied that writing would be his major. This involved three semesters as editor of *Kodon,* the campus magazine.

"The only way to get an A in this class is to have something published," Dr. Walker told his eager young scribes.

The challenge was accepted. Larry secured his A when he wrote an article on "Unbelievable Bud" Schaeffer, a Wheaton basketball star, for *Power* magazine and another for *My Counselor,* both published in Chicago by Scripture Press.

By the next year of school, Larry and Lorraine were married. While carrying a full scholastic load, he served as pastor of the Michigan City, Indiana, Missionary Baptist Church (General Association of Regular Baptists), traveling the two hours by train every weekend with his bride, and on other occasions as he was needed. In addition he accepted a position as Managing Editor of *Christian Life* magazine (alternating work days with Alvera Johnson, who was leaving the position to teach at Wheaton). Larry also took night classes in journalism two nights a week at Northwestern University's Medill School of Journalism, and later in layout and design at the American Academy of Art in Chicago.

William J. Petersen, editor of *Eternity* magazine, entered Wheaton College two years behind Larry.

"I walked into the office of *Kodon* magazine," he says, referring to the campus literary journal, "and met the stocky, cheerful editor. Larry took me under his wing, encouraged me, counseled me, bolstered me. Before I knew it I was an assistant editor of the magazine.

"Larry has always been a great encourager. I was amazed that this upper classman who was really a big man on campus cared about me and my future. Beyond that, he had a

73

contagious excitement about Christian journalism.

"He was a tireless worker. He would go without sleep for seventy-two hours to meet deadlines and prepare papers for classes. How he remained so buoyant through it all, I can't say. Then he would sack in for twenty-four hours straight to catch up.

"He and Lorraine lived in a trailer behind the men's dormitory. One night just before a deadline on the campus magazine, Larry invited me over to meet Lorraine and share dinner with them. I will never forget the simple warmth of the home and the graciousness of Lorraine.

"When our oldest son Ken was born, Larry stopped in for a fortuitous visit. I'll remember always the way that Larry prayed for the baby, who was struggling for his life at the time. Larry cared, and you felt his caring."

Lorraine worked as a nurse at West Suburban Hospital, but she kept the coffee pot filled for Larry's campus buddies, such as Henry Pucek and Bob Baker, who made regular visits.

With a full load of units at Wheaton, two nights of study each week at Northwestern University in Chicago, working three days a week at *Christian Life*, preaching each weekend in Indiana, editing *Kodon*, "doing anything anybody asked me," Larry faced in his last year of college one of life's most anguishing moments—the loss of a promised life.

"The miscarriage was a shattering disappointment," Larry and Lorraine recall. Two kids in a trailer, a long, hard night, a kind neighbor's call for an ambulance . . . finally the trip to the hospital to make certain no infection would threaten the life of the mother. But the ordeal seemed far away and finally forgotten with the appearance on June 16, 1951, of Sherilyn Sue.

As Larry's 1949 graduation day approached, the Wheaton faculty discovered that he was one unit short in the sciences. Larry enrolled for a semester of geology and went happily to the first class. "It was," he found, "so terribly boring that I didn't go back." He read the textbook, went in on the last day, took the final examination, and got a C. It was that grade which lowered him to "high honors" at Wheaton instead of the *Summa Cum Laude* distinction.

In June 1949, after graduation, Larry turned in earnest to the things God would have him do. He had learned to trust his Lord for the future because he had seen God's fingerprint on the past. He had been weighing graduate studies in either journalism or theology, and considering a "call" to serve as pastor of the church in Indiana. But then, as now, Larry was geared to meet needs. His friend and mentor Bob Walker needed someone at his side, and that was enough for Larry. The day after he graduated he reported for full-time work at *Christian Life* magazine as assistant managing editor, and shortly thereafter took the full position.

Larry was famous at *Christian Life* for his speed and accuracy in proofreading the galleys. Once when he was away on a trip he returned to a happy staff who had just put the next edition to bed at the printers. When Larry picked up a set of proofs, they assured him, "You have nothing to worry about. They've been read and reread and all corrected."

Larry let his eye travel down the galleys.

"Hey, don't you trust us?" his associates pouted.

Pretty good job . . . until he came to the last galley. There he spotted a paragraph which read: "Don't miss the followup article in the next issue by our managing editor, Larry Lard."

A quick stop-press call to the printer corrected most of the issues, but thousands were already packaged and gone, to give subscribers a good laugh.

ten
GOD'S SYNCHRONY

The world for Larry Ward during his stint in the offices of *Christian Life* on Wabash Avenue in Chicago's Loop was growing wider. The film "China Challenge," distributed by Youth For Christ Evangelist Bob Pierce, had piqued Larry's interest in missions and in the wider world of a Christian's responsibility.

Perhaps that's why a small notice in the *Chicago Tribune* which he read one morning in 1951 on the commuter train from Michigan City, Indiana, to Chicago caught his interest:

> U.S. Government wants persons for exciting experience abroad. Need journalism background.

Larry folded the paper and pondered the matter. The idea of going abroad as a missionary at the expense of Uncle Sam appealed to him. At the office he sent a note asking for an application.

Several days later a phone call invited him to the Conrad Hilton Hotel for an interview. On the day appointed he entered the lobby and found it full of hopefuls like himself. Thinking he had little chance, he waited for half an hour or so, watching the men and women enter and leave in a steady stream. He was about to leave when finally his turn came.

"We're forming an agency called 'Voice of America,'" the officer in charge explained after an hour or so of interview. The longer they talked, the more Larry warmed to the assignment. His journalism credentials and experience were especially appealing to the government, along with his high moral standards. The salary was high, the benefits plentiful. He was told there would be something like 120 days home leave each year.

"You're the kind of man we're looking for," his interviewer finally said. "Here, fill out these papers and bring them back in a week. A special committee will be coming from Washington to interview you."

Larry left thinking he was on his way, but in the week that followed he sensed in his heart a growing check against his accepting the assignment. Finally, on the day of the appointment he went early to the office. He put the sheaf of papers on his desk and wrote his name on the first line as directed. Somehow it just didn't look right. He had arranged to take the day off, but he phoned the Voice of America office at the Hilton and told the contact person that he would not be applying. He tried to explain, but his reasons fell awkwardly on unhappy ears. "I just feel God doesn't want me to do it," Larry summed up.

As he hung up the phone his secretary buzzed. "A Doctor Ketcham is waiting to speak to you," she said, "Doctor Robert Ketcham of the General Association of Regular Baptist Churches."

"We've been trying for some time to organize a publishing house for our association," the caller explained, "but we don't know anything about this sort of thing. Is it possible you could get away today and come over to give us some advice?"

Larry was confident that God had timed the call . . . and somehow he knew at once that his happy days at *Christian Life* were winding down and that a new opportunity was upon him to serve the church group in which he had found the Lord.

As Director of Publications for the GARBC, Larry began almost immediately to travel. He visited churches, talked to Sunday school leaders, interviewed Christian Education directors, and became acquainted with pastors. With travel went the joy and the fulfillment as well as the tediousness and disappointment—and sometimes the unexpected.

In Eldora, Iowa, one evening he had fielded questions at a Christian education convention and had left the pulpit. A woman approached shyly but with determination.

"Could you tell me," she began, "what a man in our church meant when he stood up and quoted the strangest verse and said it had a special meaning for him?"

"Which verse was it?" Larry asked.

"This one right here," she said, pointing to 1 Chronicles 26:18, "'At Parbar westward, four at the causeway, and two at Parbar.' Do you think the man was crazy, or just being funny, or what?"

Larry took a deep breath. "Well," he began, "I've never met the gentleman so I can't judge his mental stability or lack of it. But first, we must remember that all Scripture is given by inspiration of God—literally is 'God breathed.' It's all there—the begats, the genealogies, and even what the poet called 'Isaiah's wild prose.' It's all given for our benefit and blessing.

"Next, remember that 'the text without the context may be a pretext.' You have to find the setting of a verse before you make a decision as to its full meaning."

A small crowd had gathered by now, so Larry folded his arms, frowned with pretended erudition, and warmed to his subject with a twinkle in his eye.

"Look back about three chapters or so in 1 Chronicles where it says, 'Concerning the division of the porters.' I remember a Sunday school lesson not long ago which said there were 4,000 such porters assigned to duty in the house of the Lord. They were there to serve as guards, ushers, and sentries. So when you come to 1 Chronicles 26:18 you have 'concerning the division' or the 'establishing' of the porters. God deploys his troops. There's a sermon right there—we make ourselves available for God, and then he decides where to put us. The most important ability is availability. He puts you where he wants you. But there's more!

"What's this 'causeway' in that strange verse this man quoted? Well, 1 Kings 10 tells us that the Queen of Sheba came to call on King Solomon. We read that when she saw his house and his servants and cupbearers and the ascent by which he went up to the house of the Lord, there was no more spirit in her. 'Thy wisdom and prosperity exceedeth the fame which I heard,' the Bible says (v. 7). Notice, ' . . . and his ascent.' I understand that the ascent by which the king went up was an incredible ramp or passageway which went over the deep valley between his palace and the temple. It has been described as 'a feat of early-day engineering, one of the wonders of the world.'"

Larry continued to point out to the woman, who by now was surrounded by all the lingering parishioners, how "this verse might indeed make sense, because I believe the 'ascent by which the king went up to the house of the Lord' was this same causeway referred to in 1 Chronicles 26:18! Here you have the assignment of these porters, and four of them get to serve up here on the causeway where the king himself comes by on his way to worship three times a day! You do not serve to be seen but seen you are. Here they are when the king goes by. And with that position comes great responsibility."

Larry paused and surveyed his group. Some were smiling, others were nodding, others looked puzzled.

"Pastors, teachers, evangelists, and deacons—people like that—are up there serving on a 'spiritual causeway.' What a place of mixed privilege and responsibility! But this second reference to 'Parbar westward' seems to refer to a little ole gate which was at the back of the temple. God needs people up on the causeway where the tourists come in wide-eyed wonder . . . but he also needs people at the back door, around the corner and out of sight. He needs leaders up on the causeway, and he also needs people out of sight in their 'prayer closets.'

"A reading of the passage seems to indicate that the Spirit inspired the phrases equally. Where we serve is up to God. And look—at Parbar *westward* . . ." (Here Larry admits he might have stretched the meaning of the verse a bit.) "Their faces were turned toward the setting sun. So, whether you serve up there on the causeway, in a conspicous place of public service, in some spot of plaudit or recognition, or whether you serve around the corner and out of sight at 'Parbar'—we're all at Parbar 'westward.' Time is running out. 'The work that centuries might have done must crowd the hours of setting sun.' Let's get with it and go!"

The group had a good laugh. Some applauded. The woman closed her Bible. "Thank you," she said politely. "You've shed some light on this passage for me."

A year passed with GARBC. During that time a printer named Gerald May in Hayward, California, wanted to help his church and offered to print the educational materials. So Larry move the GARBC editorial offices from Chicago to Hayward in order to guide the printing of the denomination's editorial projects. His travels over the next three years took him to some 500 of the GARBC's 700 churches coast to coast.

A break came in 1954 when Larry, as editor of the official periodical *The Baptist Bulletin*, disagreed with an article Dr. Ketcham had written which was critical of Evangelist Billy Graham. Larry had a profound admiration for Dr. Ketcham, and respected his right to his own opinions. But he insisted such an article should be identified as from a personal viewpoint and not seem to represent an official GARBC position. (The association itself had taken no specific position on Graham and his crusades.)

Larry also had differences with his GARBC brethren

because he was not the extreme separatist many of them were; but for Larry the emotional ties remained strong. He had surrendered his life to Christ in a GARBC church in Norwich, New York. He had been licensed to preach by the GARBC at fifteen. His father was a GARBC preacher. The people in those churches loved the truth and stood for salvation—and in that he could join them.

But he felt they often attracted bad press they didn't deserve, because they let a vocal minority speak for them.

In a meeting in Los Angeles, the council of fourteen of the GARBC sided with him indirectly. In fact, they offered to create for him a new position in which he would become the official spokesman of the GARBC, and they encouraged Dr. Ketcham to use his gifts of preaching in the sunset years of his ministry in Bible conferences.

Larry was thirty-one years old. He felt honored to have this invitation from the General Association of Regular Baptist Churches. But he felt that God wanted him to remain in California, even though he didn't know exactly why. He only knew that it was time for him to resign.

In February of 1955, he submitted his resignation to the GARBC. It was accepted, but with the request that he continue in his work until June 1.

Meanwhile, in a totally unrelated development, Larry had written to an old friend—Dr. Cyrus N. Nelson, President of Gospel Light Publications—suggesting that a publisher such as GL should issue a magazine for Sunday school teachers. Larry actually proposed a specific content for such a periodical, giving it the working title of *Teach*.

This led to a continued communication with Dr. Nelson, finally leading to a letter to Larry which stated: "Gospel Light as a matter of policy doesn't hire people away from other organizations. But if you decide that you yourself would like to pursue that idea for a magazine, we would be open to talk with you about it."

In still another "unrelated" development, Larry and Lorraine had received the startling news that the property on which their house was situated in Hayward, California, had been condemned for a city parking lot. This led to a legal hassle.

Returning from the board meeting in Chicago at which he had resigned from the GARBC and had accepted the request to stay on until June 1, he found two bulky envelopes awaiting him. One was a specific job offer from Dr. Nelson. It stated: "Come whenever you like. We have discussed it here, however, and the ideal date for us would be June 1."

Larry blinked, and then breathed a silent prayer. Even the date seemed to be a confirmation of this move as in the will of God.

He opened the second letter. It was an official document, telling him that a check in a certain amount had been desposited to his account in the bank, and that this completed the purchase of his home. The letter stated: "But as a mark of good faith and to show our desire to cooperate, even though your house is now officially ours, you are free to stay there free of rent or other charge until June 1."

"It always seems that God deals with me this way," says Larry. "I guess he knows that once I *know* I am really in his will, I can move ahead with total confidence. So he seems to underscore it for me, as he did with these three items which all converged on that same day, June 1."

Larry and Lorraine, with little Sheri and Mother and Dad Hustad, purchased two houses and a garage on half an acre in Montrose, California, just north of Glendale. Now Larry took the job as director of education services for Gospel Light Publications. The year was fun, relaxed, rewarding. The Wards enjoyed Montrose, and after Larry's four years of heavy pressures, constant travel, and long days away, they found a special benediction in evenings at home together unaccompanied by a briefcase full of extra work.

Larry loved his colleagues at Gospel Light, and was privileged to serve with them in a sort of "transition" period. He took the first steps to get *Teach* underway, and spent a great deal of time in evaluating other periodicals and publications of Gospel Light and making long-range proposals.

But he was about to hear the beat of another drum.

As he walked into his office one morning in early 1956, an unmistakable feeling swept over him which was as clear as if an audible voice had said, "Your work here is ended."

He sat down weakly and propped his elbows on his desk. What was this? Lorraine and Sheri and the folks were happy here. His job was very rewarding. The salary was adequate.

If I left, Larry reasoned, *what would I do? Work on a magazine?* But then he asked himself, *What magazine?*

The urge continued. *How about a missionary society?*

In the middle of his reverie, the phone rang. "Larry, this is Carl Henry. I don't know if you remember me or not, but I'd like to ask you some questions. I'm not at liberty yet to tell you why, however."

Eventually, Dr. Henry explained: "We're thinking of publishing a new periodical. Your name has been suggested as managing editor." Carl went on to explain that they were not thinking of a person to be directly involved in the content planning of a new periodical, but to take care of the mechanical aspects of production.

Larry promised to think it over, and Carl thanked him warmly.

Leaning back, Larry thought through what his answer would be if Dr. Henry did ever call him back. His several years of directing the Regular Baptist Press had broadened his outlook and experience. Here at Gospel Light he had been involved in studies related to advertising and promotion and marketing in general. To return now to the limited work of production after all these broader areas of experience seemed unappealing. He reached for a clean sheet of paper on his desk and wrote:

1. Editorial production
2. Circulation promotion
3. Advertising solicitation

Larry slipped the note under his telephone and turned to the work of the day, thinking that if Dr. Henry did call back, he would just read the material from this note to explain his broader base of experience and why the limited responsibility of production would not be sufficiently challenging.

But now the thought had at least entered his mind that perhaps the Lord was planning for him to move on. At home that night Larry discussed the turn of events with Lorraine. "If I had my choice of where to live," he said, "I think it would be Washington, D.C. That would be a fascinating place."

The next day he drove to the post office to look at the listings of available govenment jobs. Somehow the Lord seemed to be prying him loose from his position in Glendale, one finger at a time.

A couple of weeks later, Carl Henry's voice was on the line again. Larry reached under the phone and pulled out the sheet of paper on which he had listed his reasons for not accepting the job.

"Well, Larry, the job I spoke of earlier has broadened a bit," Carl said. "I don't know whether or not you will be interested. It now covers three areas instead of just one— editorial production, yes, but also circulation promotion and the entire advertising program."

Larry listened in amazement, looking at the paper in his hand as Dr. Henry, without knowing it, quoted almost verbatim the list he had prepared.

Then a letter from Billy Graham followed, urging Larry to take the position with the new magazine.

"I have followed your career for years," Billy wrote in essence, "and I think you're the man to help us get this new magazine started."

The magazine would be called *Christianity Today,* a periodical to serve as a counterpoint to the liberal *Christian Century*. Location? The offices would be in Washington, D.C.

On his get-acquainted trip to Washington, Larry could

easily see that the other editors (basically theologians, preachers, and writers) were outstanding in their own areas but desperately needed the help of one experienced in actually putting a magazine together. He was asked to travel to New York City to be looked over by J. Howard Pew, the oil magnate who was financially backing the periodical for its first years.

The tycoon opened his suite door at the Waldorf Towers (atop the famed Waldorf Astoria Hotel) to admit Larry, took a puff on his cigar as if to say, "You're not quite what I expected," turned around, and let Larry into another room. After Mr. Pew had asked a preliminary question or two, Larry surprised himself by taking the initiative. "Pardon me, sir, but I'd like to ask *you* some questions."

J. Howard Pew laid down his cigar, blinked, and peered at him as Larry queried: "You're putting up a lot of money for *Christianity Today*. What does this mean? Are you going to dictate the editorial policy?"

Mr. Pew blinked again, looked at Larry for a moment, and then leaned back and smiled. Somehow the atmosphere of the interview changed. Mr. Pew answered the question frankly, and to Larry's satisfaction.

Looking back on that interview today, Larry wonders how he mustered the gall at the age of thirty-one to say what he did to a famous executive. But the pleasant conversation that followed rewarded him, and Larry greatly appreciated his further contacts with Mr. Pew through his career at *Christianity Today*.

The Wards leased their Montrose house for the promised year of work—April 1956 to April 1957—moved to the capital, and Larry plunged into the heavy load of editorial work. The demands were so great, the hours so long, and the pressure so intense that a skin rash appeared on Larry's arms. The loss of sleep and the relentless demands of editorial production, advertising solicitation, and circulation promotion were taking their toll.

Automobile trips with Lorraine and Sheri through the

Shenandoah Valley, the Skyline Drive, and the strategic battlefields of the Civil War provided weekend diversion. As they were passing one Saturday afternoon through Front Royal, Virginia, Lorraine exclaimed, "Did you see that sign?"

"What sign?"

"Back there, that historical marker?"

Larry put the car in reverse gear and backed up along the curb to read a message which would have far-reaching implications. It said something like this:

> On May 23, 1862, the Maryland First Regiment CSA opposed in this village the Maryland First Regiment USA. Believed to be the only time in the Civil War in which the divided halves of a single regiment fought each other.

Larry surveyed the peaceful streets, the well-kept houses, the manicured lawns of the city park. "Right here," he said, "brother battled brother . . . people who looked alike, who were raised in the same communities . . . boys who knew each other, shooting and bayonetting each other. . . ."

He shook his head to get rid of the thought. For the first time in his life the Civil War took on an atmosphere of reality, instead of just being dull history.

That night in a motel at Winchester, Virginia, he bought a book chronicling the battles of the area—the battle of Front Royal, and of Newmarket, where youthful students of the Virginia Military Institute (ages twelve to fourteen) were strapped into their saddles and thrust into the war.

"It reads like fiction but it was *real,*" Larry commented to Lorraine and little Sheri.

In the weeks following, the idea of a novel formed in his mind. He read all he could get of the life and times of Stonewall Jackson and learned that the great Confederate general was a committed Christian believer.

By dawn's early light in the weeks that followed, Larry

ground out his story of two brothers, one in each half of the Maryland First Regiment. Finally the dark, dreaded day comes and they face each other on the streets of Front Royal.

In October, just as the first issue of *Christianity Today* was to appear, Larry got up extra early one morning to write a prologue to *Thy Brother's Blood*. "Old friend fired at old friend, ex-comrade drew sword on ex-comrade—and brother battled brother. . . ."

In Larry's view, what he had written was really just an extended outline for the great historical novel that he would write "someday," when he had time to finish it.

But then, caught up in the pressures of issue after issue of the new magazine, the manuscript gathered dust in his desk and finally went with him back to California.

That was in 1956. In 1961, with the centennial of the Civil War's start only months away, Floyd Thatcher of Cowman Publications phoned Larry to have lunch.

"If I were a publisher," Larry reflected, "I'd really get on the bandwagon of the Civil War. There's going to be a lot of interest. Floyd, why don't you bring out a great Civil War novel?"

"Okay," Floyd replied, "why don't you write it?"

Larry reached into a bottom drawer of his desk, pulled out a faded manuscript in a ragged box, blew off the dust, and handed over *Thy Brother's Blood*.

Shortly after that he left for an extended trip outside the country. Opening his mail in Japan one day, he found a flyer announcing the soon appearance of the civil war novel, *Thy Brother's Blood*, by Larry Ward, the story of Stephen and Wade Andrews, one in gray and the other in blue. It would be issued on the Centennial Anniversary of the beginning of the Civil War.

Thy Brother's Blood deserves rereading, if only to understand Larry Ward better. The two brothers, Stephen and Wade, were on opposite sides in more ways than one. Stephen was a Christian; Wade was not.

In the last scene of the book, after the two have met in the heat of battle and (at the insistence of Stephen, the Christian) have actually fought each other, Wade tells what finally brought him to faith in Christ. One step was when he met Stonewall Jackson, whom he described as "a real man."

But the most convincing thing to Wade (as quoted earlier) had been the example of his own brother, a man "to whom truth was truth so much that he would pick up a gun he hated, and kill men he loved—and even fight with his own brother."

That is the same dedication to truth which has always marked the life of Larry Ward.

The year at *Christianity Today* had been another great experience for Larry Ward. He had kept his commitment to work away at those three jobs until each area had a full-time person to direct it.

But now, although he was offered even broader editorial service opportunity at the new magazine, his heart told him that God had other—perhaps different—work ahead for him.

Right on schedule the Wards returned to California. Lorraine, Larry, and Sheri—each with a keepsake first edition of *Christianity Today* in their suitcases—made their way West, back toward home, toward Grandpa and Grandma Hustad, toward new and exciting endeavors in the synchrony of God.

eleven
WORLD VISION

In his Spanish-style white house under the stately trees at 4444 Briggs Avenue in Montrose, California, Larry cleaned out a closet and put in a desk. On December 14, 1957, he would be thirty-three years old. His promised year at *Christianity Today* had ended, as had his earlier stint at Gospel Light Publications. Larry Ward was a free agent.

Even though his desk had been narrowed, his world in 1958 would stretch beyond the 700 churches of the GARBC . . . the 60,000 subscribers of *Christian Life* . . . the domain of Washington, D.C., and the new voice for the evangelical faith, *Christianity Today*.

Shortly before leaving Washington to return to California, Larry had talked with Dr. Frank Phillips, whom he recognized as the hard-driving chief executive of a missionary agency called World Vision, Inc., based in Portland, Oregon.

"Larry," said Dr. Phillips, "I hear you'll be going to Cincinnati next month for the convention of the Evangelical Press Association. Roy Wolfe, one of our staff guys, will be going too. He's kind of reserved. Would you look out for him?"

Roy, a veteran of the art staff at the *Portland Oregonian* newspaper in his home state, was seeking an editor for the publication which would eventually become *World Vision Magazine*. But Roy didn't mention his mission to Larry in Cincinnati. The two talked about generalities, ate Chinese food, and enjoyed the EPA program. Afterward, Larry returned to Washington, while Roy went to Chicago for an interview with Dr. Robert Walker.

When Roy mentioned he was in search of a top-drawer journalist, Editor Walker scratched his head. "Well," he pondered, "you might ask Larry Ward. I've just heard that Larry will be leaving *Christianity Today.*"

In the Mayflower Hotel of Washington, D.C., at a convention of National Religious Broadcasters, Frank Phillips asked the same question of *Christianity Today's* news editor, George Burnham. Just then George spotted Larry standing nearby. "There's your man!" he said. "Larry, could you come here a minute? Frank, here, is looking for an editor."

Larry smiled. "I appreciate your thinking of me, Frank, but I'm pretty well settled in the Los Angeles area with several accounts and probably couldn't move to Portland. . . ."

"You're behind the times, Larry," Frank said, laughing. "We've just moved to L.A.—1101 West Colorado Boulevard in the suburb of Eagle Rock."

"That's about six miles from my house," Larry said. "I'll come in to see you next week."

Back in his room, Frank took a call from Roy in Chicago. "I've got an editor for us," Roy reported.

"I beat you to it," replied Frank.

"Who's yours?"

"Larry Ward."

Roy chuckled. "That's *my* man, too!"

Until this time, World Vision to Larry Ward had been just Bob Pierce, a big, red-faced Youth For Christ evangelist who toured the country showing films of Asia and taking offerings for the needy. The closer Larry got to the organization the clearer the opportunities became. He worked for several months as a consultant, testing the waters, watching God's clock. He was enjoying all of his accounts, but somehow World Vision was beginning to take most of his time and creativity. Larry thrilled to its potential.

One late afternoon, December 7, 1957, he pulled a piece of stationery out of his suitcase in the offices of his client, World Vision, and wrote a note to Frank:

> You've always said to me if ever I wanted to go full time all I had to do was to notify you. Well, if you want me, here I am.

Frank, bubbly and excited, phoned as soon as he received the message. "It's all arranged," he exclaimed.

One month later Frank Phillips suffered a fatal heart attack on the steps of an airplane at Los Angeles International Airport.

The timing of that note had been strategic. Larry little knew when he wrote it how urgently Bob Pierce would need someone to move into the entire area of promotion.

The months went by, and Larry swiftly moved from serving as an editorial consultant to the big (though as yet untitled) job of coordinating all of World Vision's information and fund-raising programs. He appreciated Roy, and all his colleagues at World Vision. This happy association was enhanced by Lorraine's announcement that a second child would be born in August of 1958.

In order to clarify in their minds the scope of World Vision's projects, to capture need in thousands of photographs, and to lay the groundwork for expanding missionary projects, Larry and Roy had planned a trip that would take them around the world. The proposed itinerary with its strange-sounding names was delivered by a travel agency just in time to complicate the happy announcement.

"You'll be leaving," Lorraine pointed out, "three days after the baby is expected."

"Then I'll cancel," Larry declared.

"How can you?" Lorraine replied. "You've got all your hotel reservations, all your flights arranged. . . ."

"Honey, if you want me to cancel, I will," Larry insisted. But Lorraine was equally insistent.

On August 6, 1958, Kevin Charles Ward was born—right on schedule. And right on schedule three days later, Larry and Roy departed on an SAS flight for Copenhagen, the first leg of their momentous trip.

Does the lack of bonding between father and child in those early days and months affect their future relationship?

"We've thought about it a lot," says Lorraine. "Today we live near both of our children and have the sweetest relationships any parent can hope for. Kevin, in his growing years, when Larry was traveling so much, did have my father living in an adjacent house. Dad provided the male companionship which Kevin needed. Kevin loved Grandpa so devotedly that he even began to walk like him, limping a bit just as my dad did."

Sheri suffered most from her father's long absences during her teen years, both parents would agree. But the early associations of family living and a strong church home helped. They were enough to bring her full circle into her majority and into her present life of very active Christian service.

When he wasn't writing appeal letters, news releases, photo captions and copy for brochures, leaflets and mailing inserts, Larry was giving time to the larger strategy of World Vision, Inc. He categorized the thrust of its endeavors into five basic goals: (1) Social Welfare Services, (2) Evangelistic Outreach, (3) Christian Leadership Development, (4) Emergency Aid, and (5) Missionary Challenge.

He conceived the idea of offering with no rental fee World Vision's new film, "A Cry in the Night" to churches which promised to take up an offering for *their own* missionary outreach. The plan (despite early misgivings by Bob Pierce) was an instant success in promoting the services of World Vision nationwide.

Early breakfast appointments, after-dinner phone calls, and heaps of mail dominated Larry's schedule at home, in the office, and on the traveling circuit. Sandwiched in was the work of the Evangelical Press Association, now a decade old. Larry had agreed in 1958 to develop the weekly EP News Service, both to serve EPA's member editors and to garner needed revenue for the association's program. He created and named the bi-monthly *Liaison* news sheet which would present information and announcements of interest to the editorial family; he also wrote a yearly "Religion in Review," directed "Protestant Press Month," attended board meetings, traveled to host cities to plan conventions, and arranged for grants from World Vision to strengthen the base of EPA, which served Christian editors widely diverse in responsibilities and theological viewpoints.

"As I told Bob Walker on a train back there in 1948," says Larry, "I consider that experience with EPA—serving the field to which God called me—one of the greatest privileges of my life."

A phone call from Larry Ward in July 1958, asked if I would write the weekly EP News Service while he was overseas on that first globe-circling trip. The "account" was a glamorous one for me in my pint-sized free-lance writing career in Long Beach, California. I had been married for just two years and relished the opportunity to broaden my responsibilities. These grew broader still on November 2, 1958, when I drove up to 1101 W. Colorado Boulevard at Larry's invitation. Just as I parked my Ford across from the tiny annex, out stepped Larry Ward and Roy Wolfe from their postage stamp quarters.

"I have to admire these guys who show up for work precisely at coffee break time!" Larry teased. That was my first indication that I had the job, that we would be working together.

During the coffee break at Bob's Big Boy restaurant we turned over the table napkin and outlined the second issue of the new *World Vision Magazine.* Such a periodical is routine now for missionary agencies, but in those early days it was indeed a phenomenon. Response was voluminous.

The very first issue had been put together toward the end of that world trip in several countries of Asia. Larry wrote the copy in Manila—but where to have the type set in English? A patient search led to a Chinese printer with English type who would set the galleys and provide glossy proofs which could be pasted down for the printer's camera. Larry and Roy could discuss with him the printer's jargon only through an interpreter, so the process required many hours of patient negotiation. While Roy stayed in Manila to get the proofs, Larry went on to Taiwan where they would later meet.

Proofs in hand, Roy landed in Taipei and set about to lay out the proofs, page by page, in that hot, humid climate. All he needed were the usual tools: a board with a straight edge, a T-square, a ruling pen, a jar of rubber cement, and some cardboard on which to fasten the layouts so they would not get bent or wrinkled between the drawing board and printing press.

The only T-square was a strange variety with graduated sides sloping from its wide mount on the crossbar to a tapered end. Unless the layout was turned, all the lines of type on the page would go downhill. The only ruling pen was a left-handed type that wouldn't let the ink flow smoothly. And the only "rubber cement" available was a kind of white Formosa glue. Finding no table to accommodate his layout, Roy had to use the lid of a toilet seat—the only flat surface in their improvised production shop half a world away from the office in California.

"Those were the fun years," Larry recalls. "Roy and I believed in the program and gave ourselves to it wholeheartedly. It was gratifying to see the response."

In Larry's tiny British-built "Sprite" he would often pick me up in neighboring La Canada and we would cruise through the early morning fog, make our way into the new location of World Vision's offices at 117 East Colorado

Boulevard in Pasadena, and brainstorm yet another edition of the magazine or tackle a different editorial project. Still long before the office crew arrived would come the shout, "Hey, let's get some coffee and a couple o' dough-nuts . . . take a break."

The budget for World Vision, Inc., in 1957 was $750,000. Larry and Roy saw their efforts produce steady fruit over the next three years. The following year it grew to $2,068,000. By 1960 it stood at $2,668,000.

In 1962, toward the end of the year, Larry walked into his office and once again met that strange urging that the time had come for a move.

"Roy, come in here a minute, will ya?" he phoned.

There followed an outline of a plan to take their skills to a variety of worthwhile smaller agencies, offering to handle their total promotional package. Roy Wolfe's response: "Why not?"

The new information agency was called "TELL Services," taken from the Lord's admonition to his disciples, "Go and tell." Larry opened an office on Oceanview Avenue in downtown Montrose near his house and he and Roy set to work. As the news filtered out, agencies sought their serv-ices without their needing to advertise. No advice or counsel was withheld, in typical Ward generosity. All his life Larry had quite naturally helped writers and editors—even preachers—find places of service in the work of ministry. Over and over again he found jobs for the unemployed and stood by his friends.

But Larry did not fare well in the overburdening pressures of the two-man shop. The buck stopped at his desk and that desk demanded more hours than he had. The work was there, but the office was too small. The knowledge was available to share, but the heart of the servant was taxed beyond its ability to handle the possibilities.

In the fall of 1964, two years into TELL, the doctor diagnosed the trouble: angina pectoris. Larry prepared either to die or to become a vegetable. Roy, meanwhile, for family reasons, had decided to move back to Oregon. So TELL Services, despite its flourishing beginning, was dissolved.

"One last trip," Larry told his wife. "Let's take one last trip together."

They went 150 miles east to Palm Springs for several days of complete rest and diversion. A bit more hopeful, Larry returned home and began leafing through his mail. A letter from Wheaton College prexy V. Raymond Edman read:

Dear Larry:
I was thinking about you today. . . . Thought you might like to have this year's verse from Wheaton. . . .

Larry picked up the enclosure. It read, "For I know the plans I am planning for you, says Jehovah, plans of welfare and not of calamity, to give you a future and a hope."

Larry fastened his attention on the last few words: "to give you a future and a hope." He read it slowly, read it again, and held it in his hand as he walked around the room.

"Suddenly I felt the joy of the Lord flowing through me. A future and a *hope,* not as a vegetable but one full of hope . . . plans of welfare, not of calamity." Larry felt the strength of the Lord flooding through him and knelt by the living room sofa to thank God for the promise. When he got up from his knees the pain in his chest was gone. It has not returned. Larry accepts it with joy even though, "I don't fully understand it. I just accept it from the Lord and praise him."

Twenty-four hours later his comrade in mission, Bob Pierce, phoned Larry. The two men hadn't spoken for two years since Larry had announced his decision to leave World Vision. Larry had written Bob little notes from here and there, but the break was clean. Bob had given no response.

"Hi, buddy," Bob began. "I've just been thinking of you."

His voice was slow, faint, faraway. "I've been remembering some of the visits we had here together. Larry, we need each other. God bless you. I love you."

At the end of the conversation Larry sighed. "What a gift of God *that* was!" he told Lorraine. "If I die today, I'll be happy because any misunderstanding between us has been cleared up."

The next day was the date for an appointment with his Wheaton pal and confidant, Henry Pucek, and an attorney. The plan was to start a missionary agency and to become active again in world missions, which he had come to love. But a court schedule forced the attorney to cancel the lunch, and Larry was in when Bob Pierce called back. This time his speech was not slow but alert and full of authority.

"I've got a proposal," Bob asserted. "Now don't answer until you've thought this through."

Lord, help us! Larry groaned. *World Vision is the one place I wouldn't want to go back to. Here Bob and I have just worked things out and now I'll blow it.* But Bob pressed on. Twenty minutes later Larry's attitude began to change. *Well, why not?* He was prepared to accept Bob's invitation. *I'm free and we aren't talking about forever.*

"I know just the job and title I want you to have," Bob continued. "Come with me, buddy. Come back and work with me."

Bob, who had left World Vision a year earlier on a medical leave, phoned the board of directors from Japan on an intercom hookup. "I'm coming back!" he announced. "I'm coming back and I'm bringing Larry Ward with me to serve as my Presidential Associate."

Another and final separation from World Vision would come for Bob Pierce in 1967. Worn out physically and emotionally, Bob resigned from the presidency of World Vision. His friend Larry, as Vice President/Overseas Director, served on a special committee which would cover the details of Bob's severance arrangements.

One of Larry's key colleagues on the board of World Vision has commented how unusual it was that Larry could function on the committee as Bob's loyal friend and yet be equally fair to the organization in the awkward responsibility of arranging the details of the separation.

For his part, Larry likes to set one aspect of the record right. "Somehow the notion has persisted that Bob resigned at the request or at least instigation of World Vision. That isn't true. He and I spent many, many hours discussing it. Bob had reached a point where he himself felt that he just couldn't go on. I'll never forget how he surprised several of us—Dick Halverson, Paul Rees, Carlton Booth, and Ted Engstrom along with me—with that surprise announcement as we had dinner together one night following a board meeting.

"In the months and years that followed, well-meaning friends of Bob—probably in attempting to express their sympathy and identification with him—somehow fostered in his weary mind the impression that he had been driven out. Sometimes he gave way to raging bitterness, feeling that his life's work had slipped away from him and not always agreeing with the way it was being carried on. But the record will show that World Vision was absolutely fair, and then some, in its dealings with Bob. In his better moments, he would always admit that when he and I talked together."

On April 4, 1965, Larry wrote a letter of resignation to the EPA board of directors. The flow of services to member periodicals had dried up while he was out of the country. He wanted now to give the position of executive secretary to another. The time had come to give his full attention to the work of a man whose vision and creativity made more of an impact on his life than any other single individual, a man whose heart was broken by the things that break the heart of God.

Bob Pierce was a complicated man who knew his faults, believed that "God don't owe me nuthin'," and was prepared to give every ounce of strength for Christ and his Kingdom. That was the kind of dedication Larry could respect, and the kind of man to whom he could unhesitatingly give loyal service.

twelve
BOB PIERCE

Their twenty-year association had begun in an unlikely way. Larry drove to 1101 W. Colorado Boulevard in Eagle Rock that April morning in 1957 for his first appointment as a part-time publicist. Bob had just dismissed a key man in his film department—an action that was rare, because the president of World Vision usually left that kind of unpleasantness for staff to carry out.

Larry took a seat in a bamboo chair and sat quietly for a few minutes while Bob gained his composure. Dr. Pierce's round face was beet red; his brow was wet with sweat; his clasped hands trembled. When he finally began to talk, he obviously felt he had to explain what had just happened.

The president no doubt had been justified in what he had done, but Larry was observing carefully the drama before him. *All right, Lord,* he prayed, *if you want me to work with this man, I will. But I'm going to keep my self-respect. I'm going to keep the record clear with him . . . going to level with him on anything that needs to be said before the sun goes down each day.*

Behind the blustering Pierce facade Larry found a man with a driving burden for the lost . . . an evangelist with tireless compassion for the widows and fatherless of the world . . . a man with reckless generosity toward friends and servants of Christ around the world . . . a driven individual with incredible vision which could take the biggest plans others could plan, or the broadest dreams they could dream, and stretch them out of sight.

In the years of their association they worked, traveled, prayed, laughed, and wept together. They stood on the borders of then-closed China, where it had all begun for Bob Pierce in 1947, and they wept as they echoed the dying cry of Xavier for the China (Cathay) of his day: "O rock, rock—when wilt thou open to my Lord?"

They walked through the wall-to-wall children of Korea . . . the crowded streets of Tokyo . . . the bloody battlefields of Indochina . . . the hungry masses of Calcutta . . . the breathtaking vistas of Nepal . . . and forbidden areas of Northern India where almost no other foreigners had been allowed to go.

"I always operated on the fact that if it's breaking God's heart and you do what you can about it, God will make up the difference," Bob would say. "I have always called the difference between the utmost that a man could do, even with access to the greatest brains and the greatest science in the world, *God room*. The difference between that one-third and the two-thirds that God wants done is called *God room*. Everything else can be explained away. Man can take credit for it. Nothing is a miracle until it begins with *God room*."

Larry hears those words nearly every day of his life as he remembers his departed friend.

On Larry's office wall in Scottsdale, Arizona, is a color picture of Bob Pierce. Larry's associates know he always sits so that picture is in front of him. "If I have five people in my office for a meeting, there are really six. Bob is there, too."

Bob Pierce was a month away from his sixty-fourth birthday when God took him. In six decades-plus Bob had moved among kings and presidents. He had ministered to massed thousands in great evangelistic crusades in Asia, and to multiplied millions in North America via radio. He had seen that one little homeless girl placed in his arms by a distraught missionary become multiplied 100,000 times over through a child-care program which he initiated.

Born In Iowa in 1914, Robert Willard Pierce grew up in humble circumstances in Los Angeles. He made his committment to Jesus Christ as Lord and Savior at the age of twelve. Immediately he became an evangelist—on street corners, as well as in one-to-one contacts.

He attended Pasadena College but did not graduate. He was married in 1936 to Ruth Lorraine Johnson, daughter of Dr. Floyd B. Johnson, pastor-evangelist. He spent some time in itinerant evangelism, then joined his father-in-law in pastoral and radio ministries.

The year 1944 was a turning point. Bob met Torrey M. Johnson, who with Billy Graham and others was forming an organization called Youth For Christ. Bob directed the Seattle YFC rally, then hit the road later with the Eureka Jubilee Singers, a Black ensemble.

And 1947 was an even bigger turning point. Bob went to China under the auspices of YFC and discovered a new world. "Asia. The Orient. People. Millions of people. The Third World. A world of incredible need and suffering. A world which needed the healing, helpful, "right now" touch of Jesus Christ as well as his words of eternal truth.

In September 1950, Bob joined YFC leader Frank Phillips in forming a new organization. Appropriately, and reflecting his own enlarged spiritual vision, it was named "World Vision, Inc."

All these are facts—matters of record. But working with Bob Pierce wasn't always easy.

Before dawn one morning in Hong Kong, Larry's phone jangled him into sudden wakefulness.

"Buddy," Bob Pierce maundered into the phone, "are you awake?"

Larry glanced at the clock and muttered something appropriate, resisting the temptation to answer with the cliché,

"It's all right; I had to get up to answer the phone anyway."

"Larry," Bob hurried on, "something is wrong back home. At the office. I don't know what it is, but I want you to go back there at once. Take charge. Fire anybody, if necessary, *anybody*. Do whatever you have to do. . . ."

Larry interrupted. "Did you get a call, a cable?"

"No, nothing like that. But when I woke up just now I knew, I just *knew*, buddy, that something was terribly wrong back there. . . ."

"Bob, hang up. I'll be right over to your room."

By the time Larry reached his room Bob Pierce was pacing. His face was flushed, his fingers clenched. "Buddy, something is wrong, terribly wrong. . . ."

"Okay, Bob, I'll go home at once. Don't worry about it. Whatever it is, I'll deal with it."

Larry did not question God's right, or ability, to communicate directly. He himself has often felt strangely moved to pray for a loved one far away who later reported great need.

But Larry also knew Bob Pierce very well. He knew that in those early days of the sixties Bob's just-developing emotional problems often produced some strange reactions. He could lie in bed and call forth the dragons of his own imagination, each one larger and more ferocious than the one which had preceded it—mere figments of his imagination. So Larry decided to try a little amateur psychology on his friend:

"Bob, there's a flight home at nine o'clock this morning. No problem. I'll get on it. But before I go, there's an idea I want to try out on you. It has to do with. . . ."

At this point Larry was pushing his mind as hard as he could, hoping to come up with something which would pose a sufficient distraction for Bob to get his mind off his current problem. " . . . with—with an idea for a new TV series," he stammered.

Bob stopped pacing and turned toward his friend in

astonishment. The look said, *Buddy, here the whole world is falling apart and you're talking about a TV show?"*

Larry hurried on before Bob could interrupt: "Bob, let's plan a Sunday morning TV program which is really different. Not just a service from a church in North America, but the church around the world. You know, the Church of the Lepers in Taiwan. Or a little church in the bush of Africa. Maybe an early morning prayer meeting service in Korea—or that church you and I worshiped with in Moscow. . . ."

By now he had Bob's interest. "Yeah, Larry, that could be great. We could go right up in the hills near Puli—or out with Rochunga's people in Assam. Hey, we could film some of those churches which have grown out of Howie Moffett's hospital ministry in Taegu. . . ."

Now Bob Pierce had the floor. He had the "ball" and was beginning to run with it. For the next five minutes or so he paced the room in great excitement. "The Church Around the World. That's it! We'll take the people from North America all around the world, to see how their brothers and sisters in Christ worship—not just in Asia and Africa, but in Europe and Scandinavia. . . ."

Finally Larry interrupted him. "Well, Bob, if I'm going to catch that nine o'clock flight home, I'd better go get ready."

Bob looked at him as if puzzled. Then he shook his head. "Aw, let's not worry about it. If anything is seriously wrong, someone will call us or cable us. Forget it. Let's go get some breakfast and talk about this new TV series."

Their association lasted until 1967. Larry had become Vice President/Overseas Director and stayed on after Bob resigned to organize The Samaritan's Purse, which he directed while battling leukemia until his death in 1978.

In 1974 at the International Congress on World Evangelization at Lausanne, Switzerland, Bob Pierce introduced Larry to a gathering of clergymen and missionaries from all parts of the world. Said Bob:

"Now I want to tell you something. Larry Ward traveled

with me for twelve years. Many of the things that have been written over my name, Larry Ward wrote every word of 'em. That's a fact. Any place it says Bob Pierce, evangelist, author, et cetera, you can depend on it, about 99 percent of everything worth reading Larry wrote. God bless him.

"He loved me enough to help create that illusion that I was somebody and I love you for it, Larry—but the wonderful thing is that now one of the first men who moved into Bangladesh when other people were just thinking about it, a man who was there in minutes, almost, was Larry Ward. And he's loved by the head of state, by the man there who is in charge of relief for the whole government.

"Larry Ward has just been his backbone . . . and now he's in the midst of all this suffering in Africa. There are literally shiploads of food right now docking there, and other shiploads on the way . . . tons and tons of food going into the starving areas of Africa because Larry, the minute he heard about it, when he had to borrow money (I'll betcha—and I haven't asked him, but I'll bet he had to borrow money). If not, he put it on his credit card and asked God to help him before the bill came. But he went out and he got something going, and that's the characteristic of these two, Larry and Lorraine. God bless Larry Ward!"

Larry's skill in editorial communication had given a new dimension to the elements of authority and compassion which characterized the life of Robert W. Pierce.

Portrait of Larry Ward, painted by his artist-father, Whitney Ward.

Larry's father, Whitney Ward—entertainer, artist, writer, and eventually a devout Christian witness.

Proud member of the Norwich High football team. Football was Larry's first love—especially because of his admiration for Coach Kurt Beyer.

Back in Wheaton, Larry began a career as editor of the campus magazine, Kodon.

Larry and Lorraine Ward on Wheaton campus. Lorraine worked as a nurse at West Suburban Hospital in Oak Park, while Larry studied at Wheaton.

During his military stint in World War II, Larry became active in the Youth For Christ movement. Here he shares his testimony at the Minneapolis YFC rally. Next to him is Dr. George Wilson, now executive Vice President of the Billy Graham Evangelistic Association.

Larry Ward

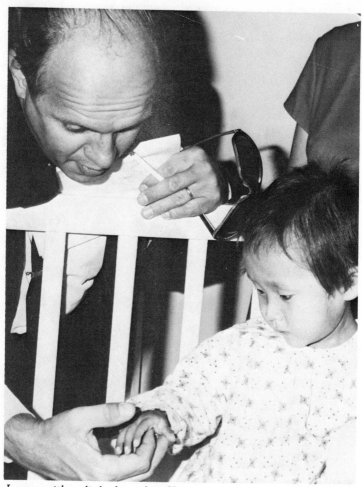

Larry with a little friend in Korea.

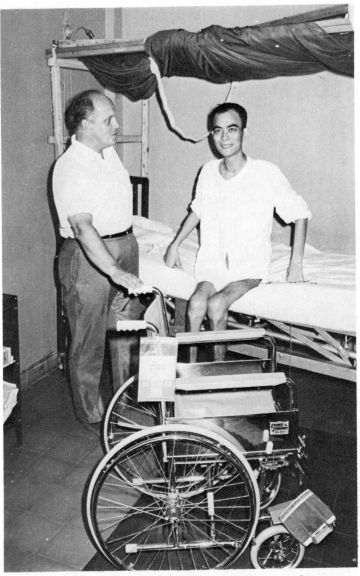

Larry during a visit to the land he loves, Vietnam. Larry was an active participant in the World Vision relief and medical programs, directed by his longtime friend, Dr. Garth Hunt.

ABOVE: *Larry has that rare ability to fall asleep anywhere. Here, he takes a catnap on a flight over the mountains of Laos.*

PREVIOUS PAGE TOP: *Larry teaches Korean children his favorite chant: "Hoo-ray for the Dodgers!" Over the years, countless children around the world have been taught this cheer.*

PREVIOUS PAGE BOTTOM: *Larry with friends, during a trip to Taiwan.*

Larry joins in a song with some Masai friends in Kenya.

Larry Ward with his beloved friend, Chaplain Warren With-row, in Vietnam.

During a rescue of Vietnamese boat people, Larry helps lift up the anchor as the Food for the Hungry mercy ship starts its voyage into the South China Sea.

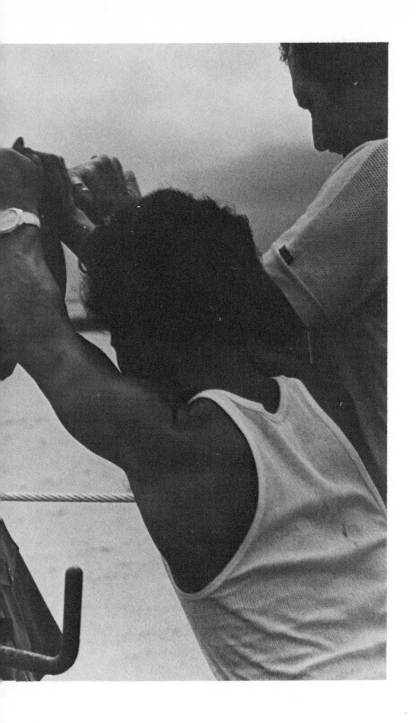

Larry helps direct relief operations in Guatemala.

Larry Ward makes an urgent TV appeal, amidst the rubble of an earthquake.

Larry Ward with refugee children in Somalia.

Many famous lives have touched his. Larry and Lorraine Ward visit with Mother Teresa in Calcutta.

High up on the roof of the world, Larry Ward visits Lake Titicaca in Bolivia.

Larry Ward and successor as President of Food for the Hungry, Dr. Tetsunao Yamamori.

thirteen

"IF YOU DRAW OUT YOUR SOUL TO THE HUNGRY..."

By 1970 Larry's mission had taken him millions of miles visiting more than sixty countries. Often he would meet with World Vision staff members and visit projects in one country by day, then board an airplane and sleep in his clothes en route to the next country and a new set of responsibilities.

Then he would carry back to North America the missionary challenge which he would use in speaking engagements, telling what still needed to be done for the poor and suffering.

Larry found the words of Jesus blunt and direct regarding a believer's responsibility to the destitute so he had no reluctance in asking for help.

A trans-Dominion speaking tour of Canada took him finally to Toronto in April 1970, where he was invited to appear on Elwood Glover's daytime television show, "Luncheon Date." When the red light of the camera came on, Glover told the audience, "Ten months out of the year the man beside me walks through a very different world from the one we know here in Eastern Canada. Today he's going to tell us about it." Then, turning around to his guest, he said abruptly, "What's the first thing you think about when you think about that world?"

Larry paused for a second, then replied: "I see an old

woman beside the railroad tracks in India. She looks like she is starving to death—and the baby in her arms could already be dead."

How strange of me to say that! Larry thought. But he hurried on, "I see a little girl in Laos, hungry. . . ."

When the red light went out Glover shook his head. "Man, you're really informed about this issue of world hunger."

Larry mumbled something in response, but all the way back to his room and into the night he pondered those words: "world hunger. . . ."

A week or so later, back in his own house in California, he dreamed that he was looking into the faces of the 12,000 people who were at that time starving to death each day. He awoke shouting, his voice ringing eerily through the house.

Strange, he thought.

The words of Dr. Richard C. Halverson, chairman of the World Vision board of directors, kept coming back to him. Larry remembered how his friend Dick had spoken strongly in a board meeting about "the world's biggest problem in the years ahead—hunger."

In Japan, on the way home from troubled Laos, Cambodia, and Vietnam, Larry was temporarily stranded for a day before he could board his flight home to the United States. He checked into the airport hotel at Tokyo's Haneda Airport, planning to dictate reports and correspondence related to his trip.

The growing burden for a hungry world kept intruding, interrupting his thoughts, demanding attention. He tried reading his Bible, but found concentration difficult. He laid his Bible down and knelt beside his bed in prayer.

"About all I could do in my prayer," he said later, "was admit to God that the great overwhelming burden for a hungry world—which so long and so slowly had been forming in my heart and mind—had now suddenly crystallized into something specific, sharp, prodding."

Getting up from his knees and sitting at his hotel desk,

Larry tried once more to resume his work. He pulled toward him the Bible which he had been reading and continued where he had left off. The words of the next verse seemed to reach out and grip him with paralyzing strength:

"And one of them . . . stood up . . . to predict by the Spirit that a great famine was coming."

The prophecy was specific in its context, but for Larry the passage of Scripture had a larger meaning—a call to involvement, a kind of confirmation that a new direction had entered his life. He could not know at that time that the burden would mean a change in his life's work, leaving an organization with which he was happily engaged, to move out alone in the vast and frightening stretches of the hungry world. He did the only thing he could think of, which was to kneel down beside his bed and pray, "Here am I, Lord, send *me.*"

In Calcutta a few weeks later as he checked into the old Great Eastern Hotel downtown, he was moved to share his growing concern about world hunger with his former associate, Roy Wolfe. That message on tiny gray stationery was the first formal crystallization of his burden to concentrate on feeding the hungry—a mission which few agencies at that time were carrying out with any regularity or emphasis.

I owe it to you, Roy, to enlarge on my thinking a bit . . . although in so doing I must not cramp your own objectivity and creativity.

I visualize: (1) An all-out campaign, alerting Christians to world hunger and informing them of their special responsibility. (2) An all-media information program, including a magazine—a "Fotomagazine." We gave the world MAP Miniature Magazine. This new format, which no one is utilizing, would be all photos. (3) Public speaking (churches, schools, service clubs). With unusual visuals and sound effects. (4) Articles

111

and releases. (5) Direct mail, of course. (6) Public service advertising. Maybe at least related to "World Hunger Day" or to our use of Thanksgiving. This includes public service radio and TV spots. (7) A film— twenty-one minutes, no narration. Music and effects. Each year Thanksgiving will be especially utilized.

All that is just the beginning. The program itself includes development of a "World Food Bank" (which is really just a computer showing available food reserves worldwide) . . . emergency aid . . . development of pilot projects and food factories worldwide, including scholarship grants . . . and cooperation in long-range technological research (really just a computerized list of research projects in action).

The Emergency Aid aspect features local-level projects as well as money. (In the spirit of our Lord's words, at the feeding of the multitude: "Give them something to eat yourselves." They had offered money!)

I am in process of listing every verse in the Bible dealing with this subject. What an eye-opener! (And heart-opener.)

Well, there she is . . . in great confidence to you alone. (No one else has heard the full vision.) What think ye? Please write about this when you get time, busy buddy. Thanx.

On each flight from then on Larry would scribble a note to Roy on the unlikely stationery of air-sickness containers and mail them to Roy at the *Seattle Times*.

I'm ready to give my life to this as Laubach did to literacy. Five years from now, the starvation problem in the world will be so big and real that most of our other problems will be seen as the trivia they are.

In another note written aloft Larry confided:

> Years and years of burden and heartache all have
> come to a special focus—the hunger problem of the
> world.
>
> I found myself preaching it over and over during a re-
> cent three-week swing of Canada. I have studied this
> thing—am writing a book using the words of Jesus, *"I
> Was Hungry"* as the working title. . . .
>
> Twenty, thirty years from now, things could be better.
> There are 48,000 scientific projects underway, trying
> to make foods out of non-foods as well as to increase
> food production. But tomorrow ten thousand people
> now alive will be dead from starvation. . . .
> Technology can help long range. But now—this year,
> next, for the next five or ten or *fifteen* years—the only
> answer lies in sharing . . . and the logical people to
> whom to tell this are the Christians (whose Lord was
> blunt and specific in his instructions).

One air-sickness bag reflected back on that first world trip
he took with Roy:

> You know, just twelve years ago right now you and I
> were pushing around out here . . . twelve years later
> the job still isn't done. The doers (Lil Dickson, Mrs.
> Donnithorne, etc.) are all older and very few new
> doers to be seen.

On September 1, 1970, only a few weeks before he
would resign from World Vision, he wrote from Seoul:

> Seems to me, Roy, that one of the things I must study
> is the complex matter of national economics vs.
> humanitarianism concern. Hundreds of thousands

starve in India while grain enough to feed them all is stacked high on the plains of Alberta. . . .

And four days later, on a flight from Phnom Penh to Bangkok:

> Yesterday I visited a Cambodian refugee center. Heartbreak. Little kids *dying* of dysentery—because they are so weakened by long-term malnutrition. Others with all the telltale signs of protein deficiency. And ahead for Cambodia—a possible serious food crisis. The areas which have supplied much of the food are under Communist control, so this can be a very critical time. Good meetings with the Ministers of Health, Social Welfare, and (re. refugee housing) Public Works. . . .

On the last leg of his journey home he wrote a brief note to Roy on an Air Vietnam motion sickness bag. The last line of the message reads, "I feel as though I am embarking on the biggest mission of my life."

Flying back to Nairobi in a small plane after visiting famine areas in Northern Kenya, Larry scribbled these lines for me on a notepad:

> *Praying with Our Tears*
>
> *Hungry and hurting,*
> *Ready to die;*
> *Hungry and hurting,*
> *Please hear my cry.*
>
> *Forty thousand children*
> *dying every day;*
> *Is anyone listening*
> *to hear us when we pray?*

Hungry and hurting,
Trying to hide our fears;
Hungry and hurting,
Praying with our tears.

Forty thousand children,
Too weary to have fun;
Forty thousand children,
Dying one by one.

fourteen
THEY DIE ONE AT A TIME...

"But Jesus said, 'You feed them'" (Mark 6:37, TLB).

In September 1970, Larry submitted his resignation to the World Vision board of directors just after he had received a raise in pay. In his new mission he would work for two years without a salary. His vast project was not begun with small plans. He was prepared to pay the price of venture.

A man is not what he does, except perhaps in the case of Lawrence Edward Ward. He doesn't ride horses, collect stamps, play golf, tennis, or even checkers. There is no greater recreation to the man who lives for others than to tackle the impossible—such as a family planning program for Calcutta, a water purification project in Africa, or a radio/television series calling affluent Americans to pay attention to the needs of his adopted people.

In 1970 World Vision invited a roomful of Larry's closest friends in Pasadena for a dinner celebrating the beginning of his new work. The agency presented to him the first gift—a $25,000 grant with which to purchase food and help ship it.

Every move Larry has made has been a step backward in terms of salary, but God always made up any lack: from *Christian Life* to the General Association of Regular Baptists; from the top editorial position with the GARBC to a slot in the editorial mills of Gospel Light Publications; from a top editorial position with *Christianity Today* to free-lance work. From working with many clients to a single one—World Vision, Inc. And finally, from a secure, well-paying position to no salary at all.

To prepare at age forty-five for a new career with a single focus and a sharpened vision, Larry turned over several small libraries. Among the first soul-wrenching volumes (there is nothing casual about world hunger) was the account of a British Methodist missionary to Africa.

"The other day a Zambian dropped dead not a hundred yards from my front door," wrote Colin Morris in *Include Me Out* (London, Epworth Press, 1968). "The pathologist said he'd died of hunger. In his shrunken stomach were a few leaves and what appeared to be a ball of grass. And nothing else."

The experience, Pastor Morris said, stabbed his conscience awake. "Two thousand years of Christian history were blown away by the faint sigh of that little man's last breath. . . . He died without knowing that Jesus cared for him, not in a sentimental, spiritualized way, but by the offer of a square meal."

Soon after that experience a periodical arrived in Zambia from the missionary's denomination setting forth an issue that suddenly had become trivial. Thundered Morris: "I don't care where they put the words of absolution as long as there is some place in the service at which I can unload my conscience overburdened with the knowledge of what we have done with that man with the shrunken belly in the name of Christ!"

Other books which Larry sampled, chewed, and digested in those days include: *The Hungry Planet,* by Georg Borgstrom (Collier); *Famine in Retreat,* by Gordon Bridger and Maurice de Soissons (Dent & Sons); *The Black Book of Hunger,* by Josue de Castro (Beacon); *Overcoming World Hunger,* by Clifford M. Hardin (Prentice-Hall); and many others. One that especially touched him was *The Social Conscience of the Evangelical*. It was written by Dr. Sherwood E. Wirt—then editor of *Decision,* and later to become a valuable member of the board of directors of Food for the Hungry.

In 1973 Larry wrote *And There Will Be Famines* (Regal Books). In the foreword Billy Graham hailed it as a book "to quicken the social consciousness." The book ends with the observation, "They die one at a time . . . so we can *help them* one at a time. And we must."

The origin of that phrase is traced to those early days when the call first came to Larry to dedicate his remaining days in the feeding of starving people. He was driving on a Hollywood street, praying aloud, "just talking with God as I drove along," and the devastating thought of more than ten thousand people dying each day from starvation or malnutrition weighed heavily upon his soul.

But Father, he prayed, *what can I do? I'm just one person. . . .*

An answer that was audible only to the ears of his heart struck him as clear as a bell: "But they die one at a time, my son, *they die one at a time.*"

Larry slowed his car, pulled over to the curb of Franklin Boulevard, and stopped. With his head bent over the steering wheel he prayed, "Thank you, Lord. If they die one at a time, then we can *help* them one at a time."

And he has.

After his resignation from World Vision but before its effective date, Larry, with son Kevin at his side, was traveling across the Pacific. Anxious that both Kevin and Sheri understand his motivations in leaving World Vision, a work in which they had shared his deep personal interests, Larry had determined to let eleven-year-old Kevin help him find a name for the new work into which God was calling him.

"Kevin," said Larry, "you and I are a special committee to find a name for this new work."

Together they sat writing various words: world, food,

hunger, and so on. Suddenly, on the Continental Airlines flight, a stewardess came by to serve lunch. Beside each plate was a small, colorful card which the airline had thoughtfully provided as a "grace before meal."

"Kevin," said Larry, "let's read this before we pray."

The words were from Psalm 146, and as Larry read aloud he suddenly came to these words: "I am the Lord who gives food to the hungry."

They both looked at each other, startled.

"Dad!" exclaimed Kevin. "That's it! Food to the Hungry!"

"How about, 'Food *for* the Hungry'?"

"Great!" Solemnly father and son shook hands . . . and Food for the Hungry has been, ever since, the appropriate name for the work which Larry heads.

And it was appropriate that the name came from the Scriptures. Like the Bereans, Larry searched his Bible to learn what it had to say about hunger. He thought he knew the Old Book, but suddenly there were more direct, piercing orders from the Creator to feed the hungry and to share with the needy than he had ever seen before.

Early in the work of Food for the Hungry, launched in January 1971, Richard Dalrymple of the *Los Angeles Herald Examiner* interviewed Larry for an article. He researched his subject, and began: "I suppose you have looked into the faces of more hungry people than any other man of our day. I guess that's why you are doing what you are now, to begin such a work to help the hungry."

"That's part of it," Larry admitted. "I would not want to look into all those hungry faces and not be moved." But now he reached out and held up his Bible. "Actually, it was not so much looking into all those faces as into this Book which gave me the incentive for what I am doing."

And this was literally true. Following the example of his own father, who so shortly after his conversion learned to search the Scriptures, Larry had gone to the Book to find out what he was supposed to do. He was particularly concerned about the priorities of his life. Those long years before, at LeTourneau Christian Camp in New York State, he had dedicated his life to Christ. He knew this meant that he would have to share the love of Christ, and point people to the only Savior of the world. He didn't want to be sidetracked by secondary issues.

But is helping the hungry a secondary issue?

Larry doesn't think so. He often says that his study of Scripture convinced him that God's love reaches out not only to the whole world but to the whole man. God cares about every aspect of our lives.

Larry's Bible is marked throughout with the letters "S J" in the margin. They stand for "social justice," which Larry feels is the bedrock of all that Food for the Hungry is endeavoring to do.

Among the verses so marked in his Bible are these:

"If I have hurt the poor or caused widows to weep, or refused food to hungry orphans . . . or if I have seen anyone freezing and not given him clothing, or fleece from my sheep to keep him warm, or if I have taken advantage of an orphan because I thought I could get away with it . . . let my arm be torn from its socket! Let my shoulder be wrenched out of place! Rather that than face the judgment sent by God" (Job 31:16-23, TLB).

"He who shuts his ears to the cries of the poor will be ignored in his own time of need" (Proverbs 21:13, TLB).

"You must love and help your neighbors just as much as you love and take care of yourself" (James 2:8, TLB).

There are dozens and dozens of such verses marked in Larry's Bible, and he has often thought about compiling them into a special condensed and topical scriptural booklet.

Events began moving rapidly in 1971. Larry's Wheaton College buddy, Henry A. Pucek, retired from the Conciliation Court in Los Angeles, rented an office twice the size he would need in the Los Angeles suburb of Eagle Rock and shared the space and rent with the new agency. A board of seven directors assembled for the first time on January 25,

1971. Attorney John Caldwell drafted the incorporation papers for the new organization. Computer genius David Tuttle (one of those first board members, "a visually handicapped person with incredible vision") offered helpful organizational counsel.

In sequential board meetings Larry charted the organization's steady growth. One of his earliest trips was to the new nation of Bangladesh (formerly East Pakistan). He was convinced as he stood at the battered airport in Dhaka early in 1972 that he had gone there "in the will of God." All around him were the ravages of war. Bangladeshis, on whose backs the people of West Pakistan for so long had grown rich, had only a few hours earlier organized their own government as the newest (and eighth largest) nation in the world. Larry felt keenly the incredible sychronization of God's purpose in bringing him to the scene at that critical hour.

"But there I stood," he recalls, "scared to death. All alone. Empty-handed. Ready to run. Some three million people had died the year before. Ten million who had walked a trail of tears to India were now coming home—in rags and poverty, many of them to find that not only had their homes been destroyed, but their villages had been completely obliterated. Tall grass covered all traces of previous habitation. An additional twenty million other Bangladeshis could be classified as refugees, displaced within their own countries."

Larry looked at his watch. Despite that whisper of the Holy Spirit he had heard at home, that sense of divine timing which had seemed so unmistakable, he thought, *Well, nothing I can do here. Might as well catch the plane to Calcutta. This is too big for me.*

Four hours later he was sipping tea there in the capital city of Dhaka in the house of the new President of Bangladesh. God arranged it after Larry made one visit to the house of Cal and Marion Olson, missionaries with the Assemblies of God who had stayed on through the dreadful nine months of war. Their lives had been preserved, but they had been robbed at gun-and-dagger point.

Larry spent most of 1972 in Bangladesh, specifically working in connection with a massive airlift directed by his friend Russell O'Quinn, a pilot who had flown help to Biafra in the earlier crisis. "The program was not without its problems," Larry recalls, "but well over twenty million pounds of rice were carried to the needy." (This was also the point at which Hollywood actress Tippi Hedren joined the ranks of Food for the Hungry, and she has been a tireless overseas volunteer ever since—distributing food in disaster situations, serving on the Food for the Hungry mercy ship in the South China Sea, and living for weeks in a tent on the Cambodian border.)

The need for an airlift had been one of the special concerns that Larry had taken to the U.S. after his meetings with the Bangladesh officials, and Russell O'Quinn had been one of the first people he called, along with Dr. J. Raymond Knighton of MAP and Dr. Viggo Olson.

In fact, Larry had called every agency that he could think of, appealing for them to move in to help Bangladesh and all its need. A particular concern was the estimated 200,000 women who had been raped by the invading soldiers of West Pakistan in what the President of Bangladesh described to Larry as "a deliberate program of national humiliation."

Just as 1972 was passing on into history, there came another disaster—the earthquake in Managua, Nicaragua. Within hours Larry was on his way there to research the needs firsthand after the massive earthquake had killed more than 8,000 people and rendered some 365,000 homeless in a few seconds of midnight terror.

Again Larry had seen God's wonderful timing. Strong headwinds had delayed the little plane in which Larry was riding to Nicaragua with his friends Dr. C. Mervin Russell, Dr. Hal Stack, and Kenneth Stroman. But, arriving with providential timing in the middle of the night, they were taken directly to the presidential palace. The young man who just "happened" to meet them in the middle of the night was the nephew of the president, and they were not only able to assess the needs, but to make arrangements so that every ounce of the 405,000 pounds of food shipped into Nicaragua by Food for the Hungry would reach the Christian workers for whom it was designated and who in turn would pass it on to the neediest of the needy.

In the months which followed, Food for the Hungry continued to send help to Nicaragua. In July a phone call from Washington, D.C., brought a message from the office of Doug Coe of the international prayer breakfast movement: "Doug phoned in from Romania. He has just been in Africa—wants to know if you have any plans to be there. He especially wants to urge you to go to Mauritania."

Larry looked at his desk and shook his head in wonderment. Sitting there was a just-delivered ticket to West Africa including a stop in *Mauritania*. Earlier that same day Larry had told his travel agent: "Pearl, work out whatever you can for Senegal, Mali, Niger, and Upper Volta. But whatever you do, make sure I get to Mauritania. My instincts tell me it has to be the hardest-hit area (with the least help) in all the Sahel."

Ten days later he had surveyed the needs and was hurrying home to rally help, to plead for food and funds. But a late arrival in Paris caused him to miss a plane. He would have to waste many hours and spend the night. Apparently he and his fellow passenger would lose valuable time.

"Well, Lord," Larry sighed, "guess I can't complain. Your timing has been so perfect these past few weeks."

Larry thought back to his earlier conversation with that companion, an agnostic pilot friend. Hank had scoffed when Larry competently predicted before the trip began that God would be going ahead of them to prepare the way. "Hank," said Larry, "mark my words. You are going to see things happen in the next two weeks which defy all the laws of chance and probability. You are going to see how God is timing our trip minute by minute and step by step."

Later that first day, as they flew toward Africa, Larry had read these words: "Oh, how great is your goodness to those who publicly declare that you will rescue them" (Psalm 31:19, TLB).

"Well, Lord," Larry had sighed, "I guess that's what I have done. I have publicly declared that you are going to rescue us!"

Now, there in Paris, he was waiting and praying when suddenly a bus appeared. *A bus? Just for my friend Hank and me? Just for the two of us?*

No, just before the bus pulled away from the curb an African gentleman hurried aboard.

"You have come far?" he asked casually, arranging his baggage.

Larry nodded. "from Mauritania . . . place called Nouakchott."

The man whirled around in delight and astonishment. "Then you must be Dr. Larry Ward of Food for the Hungry!" he exclaimed. "I missed you in my country, and wondered as I flew here today how I could contact you. I am the Ambassador of Mauritania to the United States. I have wanted to talk to you about the needs of my country, and how you can help."

"This poor man cried" in Paris . . . and time was saved, not lost. Hundreds of thousands of pounds of food were rushed to desperate people in Mauritania, because of that "chance" meeting with a remarkable man, the distinguished ambassador.

In January 1976, Larry stopped in Guatemala City to meet with Captain Jose Umberto Fuentes Soria and his associates in disaster relief coordination.

"What plan do you have," Larry asked, "for evacuation and feeding in the event of a major earthquake or volcanic eruption?"

The men smiled. "Dr. Ward, there is little chance of that here. We don't have earthquakes in Guatemala. But, yes, we do have a plan."

They produced that plan, and the meeting continued with specific discussion of how Food for the Hungry could cooperate in the event of a major disaster. That same day Larry appointed the Rev. Isai Calderon as honorary director of Food for the Hungry/Guatemala. He also phoned his office in the States to order an immediate food shipment.

Three weeks later to the day—on February 4, 1976— Guatemala City was hit with one of the most devastating earthquakes in human history. But Food for the Hungry had already shipped in 65,624 pounds of food . . . had already established top-level contacts . . . and already had its own infrastructure in place so the agency could put its relief goods in honest Christian hands for effective person-to-person distribution.

Even *before* "this poor man cried," the Lord had heard him.

In travels oft . . . in endless meetings . . . reading . . . writing reports . . . speaking and seizing every opportunity to learn, Larry spearheaded the steady expansion of Food for the Hungry into agri-research, dramatic water-purifying projects, hydroponics, irrigation, mud stoves, solar cookers, harnessing of the wind, catching and using rainfall in simple dams and cisterns. He led in the purchase and development of the Desert Center (a unique research and demonstration facility) near the newly expanded office in Scottsdale, Arizona. He also challenged his associates to develop the International Hunger Corps, a division of Food for the Hungry, training and deploying volunteers from many lands as well as the United States.

In addition to initiating the Desert Center in Arizona, he has also sparked development of an experimental ranch in Mexico for finding appropriate technology in tropical agriculture; and of an urban agricultural center in India, seeking ways in which every flat rooftop and every corner of a room can be turned into a source of food.

Larry doesn't pretend to be a technical expert. "I just see the needs out there and 'holler' for help," he says. He pays grateful tribute to his colleague Dr. Dean Nauman, who has designed most of the innovative development tools, such as solar cookers and the "Hope House" emergency shelter.

With his colorful colleague Dulal Borpujari, Senior Vice President, Larry has sparked Food for the Hungry participation in unusual seminars and workshops abroad. The agency has teamed with the Food and Agriculture Organization of the United Nations (FAO) to co-sponsor international workshops in Malaysia, China, and the Philippines on such subjects as "preserving the rice harvest" and "utilization of agricultural wastes for energy in rural food production."

Larry has been a compassionate voice to "plead the cause of the poor and needy." But his strong interests in development, in helping people help themselves, have led to the establishment by Warner Southern College in Florida of the "Larry Ward Chair of International Development." This began in the fall of 1983.

In between emergency trips abroad at times of sudden disastrous calamities or to combat creeping devastation and "desertification," he has hammered out the concept of internationalization. Larry directed the establishment of Food for the Hungry's International Coordination Center in Geneva, Switzerland, and with it the International Institute for Relief and Development (I.I.R.D.).

The I.I.R.D. provides fellowships and scholarships honoring people who have served the poor and hungry of the world . . . offers intern field experience . . . funds and participates in special undergraduate and graduate study programs . . . arranges international university exchanges . . . utilizes the help of specialists as "On-Call Fellows" . . . maintains a resource library . . . and produces various training materials.

It has specific hunger awareness tasks, such as an annual listing of the "hungriest nations" . . . the sponsorship of conferences and workshops on critical issues . . . special publications, including the *Hungry Nations Yearbook* . . . news briefings . . . and special tours for writers and editors.

"I regard the Institute as one of the most significant ventures into which God has ever led us," says Larry Ward. "We had the privilege of being something of a pioneer in the field of helping the hungry. Other fine agencies were doing that as *part* of their programs, but to our knowledge we were the first to be directly operational with this as our one specific goal and purpose, the one string on our guitar. Now we are moving on into another pioneering area, and I believe that the establishment of the International Institute for Relief and Development is fully as important as the beginning of Food for the Hungry itself."

Joining Food for the Hungry International as Executive Vice President and Director of the I.I.R.D. is Dr. Homer Dowdy, a college contemporary of Larry's at Wheaton. He is an experienced editor and writer, author of several missionary classics, as well as a leading newspaper editor, and for years an executive and eventually Senior Vice President of the Charles Stewart Mott Foundation, one of the leading and most prestigious philanthropic organizations of its kind in the United States.

"Homer is a gift of God to us," says Larry Ward. "He spent two years looking us over, secunded to us without any cost whatever by the Mott Foundation. We were honored that he had chosen Food for the Hungry for this, and then even more so when he agreed to come on board with us in a full-time position."

"Imagine," says Larry, "a Christian board sitting every three years in Geneva sponsored by the International Institute for Relief and Development—talking not only about the problems but also about the solutions . . . pointing to appropriate technology that is practical . . . educating through videotape, lectures, seminars, and workshops . . . publishing books and periodicals and 'how to' pamphlets—stocking a library of up-to-date monographs prepared by specialists in every discipline and by people of God who can expound the Scriptures and put the message of the Bible into perspective for this generation."

God's synchrony has become a way of life. It allows Larry to sleep well at night, content to let God be God in the ordering of his work.

Larry is deeply grateful for the donors who make possible all the ministries of Food for the Hungry. "We're just a switchboard," he often says, "connecting people on this end who care and share with the desperate needs out there. Here are people I don't know personally, people who don't know me except from mail or TV—but they trust us to be their hands to help the hungry. What a sense of responsibility that gives us."

While 85 to 90 percent of Food for the Hungry income is sent in "a few dollars at a time" by the general public, Larry and his associates pay special tribute to their friends who periodically help with large gifts for special needs. In addition to many such individuals, they mention especially the organizations headed by Pat Robertson, Jerry Falwell, David Mains ("Chapel of the Air"), and Val Hellikson and Paul Evans ("Haven of Rest").

"Pat, for example," says Larry, "has periodically come through with just the right amount needed at that time—often without any special appeal from us. He must really have his antenna up and pointed in the right direction—must really be responding to the Holy Spirit's guidance—for the perfect timing has been incredible. We are most grateful for people like this, who have their own big programs to support, but who stretch their hearts to help us help the hungry and homeless."

fifteen

A LIFELONG LOVE AFFAIR

"If you could choose where you were going to die, what place would it be?"

We were traveling together somewhere in Asia when I put that question to Larry Ward. Without the slightest hesitation he answered, in one word: "Vietnam."

I suspect that Larry in answering might have been remembering one or more of those several times when he did look death in the face in Vietnam during its "thirty years and thirty days of war."

Perhaps he was remembering the note he wrote to Lorraine in the dying hours of South Vietnam, in 1975. "By the time you read this, I will have been officially listed as dead or missing. Don't worry. It is all part of a plan. Unless you see incontrovertible evidence that I am dead (such as actual identification of my body) or some official notification from North Vietnam that I am a prisoner, just trust God that I know what I am doing—and that this had to be done."

To Larry Ward, this was no foolhardy adventure. He loved his family, and ached with lonesomeness at the moment he wrote those words. But his great love for Vietnam—and a deep (and, he felt, God-given) concern for Americans missing in action—were what prompted this very deliberate move.

Vietnam was just one of many countries that Larry visited on his first trip around the world with Roy Wolfe in 1958. But it was a case of "love at first sight"—and that love was to become a lifelong affair.

To Larry, Vietnam itself has always been one of the most beautiful places in the world—lush tropical settings; hundreds of miles of sparkling beach; above all, the rugged beauty of the Central Highlands.

But to a "people person" such as Larry, its real beauty was its people.

There were of course its missionaries, primarily from the Christian and Missionary Alliance (CMA) and (later) the Southern Baptists and Assemblies of God. Larry unhesitatingly describes them as "some of the greatest missionaries in all the world, some of the most wonderful people I have ever met."

One of the first people he met was John Newman, missionary with Overseas Crusades who was working closely with the CMA. Years later John was to play a large role in Larry's continuing efforts to help Vietnam by serving on the Food for the Hungry mercy ship rescuing Vietnamese boat people in the South China Sea.

Through John, Larry and Roy on that first trip met Herb and Lydia Jackson, pioneer missionaries to Vietnam who had been the first to carry the gospel to the tribal people (dubbed "Montagnards"—mountain people—by the French). Larry says, "I have no words in any way adequate to describe Herb and Lydia. Herb is one of God's noblemen—and in Lydia he has a wonderful counterpart."

And through Herb and Lydia Jackson, early in his days in Vietnam, Larry met a remarkable man named Sao A who was to become the subject of the book *The Bamboo Cross*, written by Dr. Homer Dowdy. (Sao A himself was to have a special influence on Larry's life in the years that followed, especially through his sons Ha Johnny and Ha Jimmy. And, as mentioned before, Homer Dowdy was to become a valued colleague, the executive vice president of Food for the Hungry International, and director of its International Institute for Relief and Development.)

On one of those first visits to Vietnam, Larry visited the jungle leprosarium operated by the Christian and Missionary Alliance. He came away deeply burdened for the people serving there (especially Dr. Eleanor Ardel Vietti) and for the missionaries in nearby Banmethuot, particularly Bob Zeimer, whom Larry remembers as a "rugged man's man." (It was Dr. Vietti, captured on May 30, 1962, who was to symbolize for Larry his burdens for the American missing—later also to represent those hundreds of "MIAs"—the missing American servicemen. And Bob Zeimer was to die at the hands of the North Vietnamese when Banmethuot was overrun in 1968.)

There's no way that Larry can begin to list all of the missionaries whose devotion to Christ and courage in a difficult situation impressed him so much. There were people like Grady Mangham, field chairman for the CMA in Vietnam, Pastor Gordon Cathay of the International Church in Saigon, and Dick Pendell in Can Tho.

But a very special relationship developed with a man named Dr. Garth Hunt. It was Garth Hunt who knelt beside a wounded Vietnamese serviceman, and who with tears in his eyes pleaded with Bob Pierce and Larry Ward to start a flow of crutches and wheelchairs into Vietnam—in a war marked by people maimed by land mines and grenades. And it was Garth Hunt who was to appear, driven by the constraining love of Christ in those last hours of Vietnam—to stand by Larry's side as they coordinated the exodus of hundreds of Vietnamese in those last days of April 1975. (Today Garth is a member of the International Board of Directors of Food for the Hungry.)

There were other very close ties. Two of Larry's most beloved friends were Reverend and Mrs. Jacques Mottu of Switzerland. He was the pastor of the Église Française in Saigon, serving the French community there. The Mottus stayed on after the Communist takeover in April 1975, until they were expelled fifteen months later. Now back in Switzerland, they are active in the work of Food for the Hungry International, with Jacques serving as a key advisor and Madeleine as secretary of the International Board of Directors.

While the Ward family lived in Hong Kong in 1969, they developed a close friendship with Mrs. Esther Fitzstevens, whose missionary husband John was another of Larry's special friends in Vietnam. (Today the Fitzstevenses serve with Food for the Hungry International in Switzerland, with John as Vice President/Administration in the Geneva office.)

Those were difficult days in Vietnam, and the friendships forged in the midst of the suffering were to last forever. Larry was very close to the staff of World Vision of Vietnam during his days as Vice President/Overseas Director of that organization—with special ties with Director Doug Cozart and with Relief Director Melvin Van Peursem (whom Larry regards as "one of the bravest men I've ever met"). He has warm memories of the colorful Dennis Dickerson, British-born entrepreneur/contractor, who built the World Vision complex in Saigon.

And, in a context of war in which travel was only possible through the help of the U.S. government with its planes and helicopters, he had many good friends among the American servicemen, such as Chaplain Warren Withrow and Lieutenant (now Colonel) Jim Meredith.

In one of those special circumstances which seem to characterize Larry's life—what he calls "God's marvelous timing, the synchronization of his purposes"—he encountered a young pilot named Floyd Olson. Larry "just happened" to be placed in Lieutenant Olson's bunk in Pleiku while the flyer was off on a flying mission. He noticed Bibles and Christian magazines, among them a copy of the Wheaton College alumni magazine. Later the two met, and a warm friendship developed between Larry and the younger Floyd.

It happened that Olson had been assigned his own plane, supervising control tower installations throughout Vietnam. So he and Larry were able to make many trips together up and down the country in Floyd's little "Beaver," fellowshiping in Christ and sharing some unusual experiences (such as being fired at by Charlie, the Viet Cong sniper off the edge of the Banmethuot airport).

And when Larry talks about the MIAs today, it comes very close to him. For Floyd Olson—who voluntarily returned to Vietnam the second time as Captain Olson, helicopter pilot—is one of those 2,491 still "missing and unaccounted for" in Vietnam.

But Larry also had opportunity to develop many close friends among the Vietnamese themselves. Some of his contacts were with the highest officials of the land, who remain his staunch friends today.

One of these was the Deputy Minister for Refugee Resettlement, Nguyen Van Chuc (formerly the general in charge of all engineering operations for the Republic of Vietnam). Larry's desire to help the Chuc family escape from Vietnam was the first link in the chain which formed the eventual exodus and sponsorship of more than 1,800 refugees . . . and Chuc himself, after a miraculous escape from Vietnam, joined his family in the unique "Hope Village" sponsored by Food for the Hungry in Central California in 1975. General Chuc served as the camp director, and was a strong right arm to Larry there.

And another "very, very special" friendship, to Larry, was that with Reverend Doan Van Mieng, President of the Evangelical Protestant Church of Vietnam. They had frequent contact during Larry's many visits to Vietnam with World Vision, and later after Food for the Hungry began its operations in Vietnam in 1973. Larry will never forget Pastor Mieng's heroic decision to stay on in Vietnam in the face of certain Communist takeover.

There are dozens of other names, of course, which could be listed. The people mentioned above have been isolated for special attention because—in that beautiful mosaic of God's will for Vietnam and for Larry Ward—they all play special and continuing roles.

Larry first visited Vietnam in 1958, and returned several times in the years which immediately followed.

In March 1965, he and Dr. Bob Pierce with Joe Gooden began a series of survey trips for World Vision, laying the groundwork for the massive programs of relief assistance which that organization was to bring to Vietnam in some of its darkest hours.

From March 1965 until November 1970, Larry Ward was in Vietnam for part of almost every month—traveling all through the battlefields, visiting the hospitals, meeting with government officials and church leaders, and counseling the World Vision staff as the programs developed.

His love for the country did not end when his service with World Vision was terminated. In June 1973, he returned to Vietnam to set up the country's first relief programs of Food for the Hungry, and was there frequently the remainder of that year and in early 1974.

As the end neared, he returned to Vietnam in November 1974, and was there almost constantly until April 1975. The U.S. had succumbed to political and media pressures, and had withdrawn its troops in 1972. The defenses of South Vietnam were beginning to crumble before the steady onslaughts from the north. His friends were in trouble. He would stand beside them.

What happened in those last days is related elsewhere in this book. What is worthy of mention here is the fact that Larry's love for Vietnam did not die when South Vietnam succumbed.

When opportunity came to return to Vietnam in August 1979, he jumped at the opportunity. This was the first of a series of eighteen trips over the next four years—setting up significant assistance programs in Vietnam, especially for needy and handicapped children.

It is doubtful that any other American—official or otherwise, journalist or relief worker—has had opportunity for this continuing contact with the new Vietnam. For Larry, it's simple. This is still Vietnam. These are his friends.

The love affair continues.

sixteen
"WHERE ONLY MAN IS VILE"

Larry had first gazed upon the beauties of Vietnam in September 1958, midway through its "thirty years and thirty days" of war. "Like two rice baskets at the opposite ends of a carrying pole"—that is the way the Vietnamese describe their country which uncoils in the form of an elongated S for more than 1,200 miles, from the ninth parallel north to the twenty-sixth, covering 127,300 square miles.

Vast expanses of lush vegetation and endless rice fields stretch the metallic mirror of their flooded surfaces to the horizon during the rainy season, or present the velvety green of growing rice at other times, breaking like waves upon the bony central highlands called the Annamite Cordillera.

Looking down upon beautiful Vietnam from planes and helicopters during his many mercy missions there, Larry often quoted the phrase from the old hymn, "where only man is vile." He was especially reminded of these words in early 1968.

With storm of fire the TET offensive struck Saigon and other major cities the first week of February 1968. Larry was working at home in the U.S. when suddenly a telecast was interrupted by the news that the Viet Cong had reached the guarded walls of the U.S. Embassy in Saigon and engaged the Marines in a bloody battle. To do that, Larry knew, they would have had to cross the grounds of the World Vision compound right next door. Were Doug and Linda Cozart and their children safe?

Larry grabbed the phone and called Pan American World Airways. "All flights to Saigon have been canceled," he was told. "We are over-flying until further notice."

Larry quickly explained the urgency, and was assured he would have the first available seat.

Complicated legal matters would be in question across the seas in Saigon. Stockpiles of valuable relief goods were in danger. Above all, the lives of his colleagues were threatened.

All these pressed upon him the need to go immediately into the eye of the storm.

His bag packed, Larry phoned Bert Perry, the young son of World Vision board member Coleman Perry, who had been looking for a chance to accompany Larry overseas. With Saigon still closed, they quickly booked a flight to Hong Kong, where they were told again, "all flights to Saigon are canceled and there are long waiting lists." So the indefatigable Larry made his way to Bangkok, hoping he could talk his way onto a military plane if no commercial flights were available.

His first contact in Bangkok was with the U.S. Embassy, but he didn't find it all that helpful. Larry tried to explain the urgency of the situation as well as he could, but finally gave up, feeling he really hadn't succeeded in getting his point across.

Pan American had several flights into Saigon but he was told they were military charters—reserved exclusively for service personnel.

"That's all we have," the ticket agent said, shrugging. "There's no way we can take civilians in there."

"Well, you'll need a crew, won't you?" Larry asked.

"Yes, but. . . ."

Larry clicked his heels and stood tall. "Meet your new stewardess!" he said.

The agent laughed, brought his fist down with an expletive and said, "It just might work." He reached out to shake Larry's hand. "If there's any way we can take you in, Dr. Ward, we'll do it."

Then, in order to have at least a pair of options, Larry rushed to Air Vietnam.

"I'd like to see the manager," he said to the girl at the front desk.

"I'm sorry, he's not here," she replied.

"Look," Larry insisted (a bit surprised at his own temerity), "I *know* he's here. I need to see him right now."

When the manager appeared he told Larry what he had expected: "There's nothing scheduled until further notice."

"Well then, I want to charter a plane."

"We could charter you a plane but you couldn't land," the manager explained.

"I'll take care of that. I'll get permission 'from the top' in Saigon."

The manager laughed. "Well, okay. Let's try. I'll get to work on the papers."

From there Larry rushed to a third option—the office of a Bangkok travel service. He had learned of a man with a boat (perhaps a "gun runner") who somehow went in and out of Vietnam regularly. Larry let it be known that he wanted to be smuggled in on the next trip to Vietnam. He kept retracing his steps until he became known all over town as that desperate Yankee who *had* to get to Saigon. After Saigon he was scheduled to visit Indonesia as well, so he had given his passport to the Indonesian Embassy in Bangkok.

After all these efforts, Larry returned to his hotel room just in time to pick up a jangling phone. It was the man at the U.S. Embassy whom Larry had met at his first contact but hadn't found particularly helpful. "Do you have any kind of correspondent's accreditation?" the man asked. Assured that Larry did indeed have such, the man said: "There's a special flight leaving this afternoon, taking in some news correspondents. If you can get there in twenty minutes they should be able to put you on board."

"Great!" Larry responded and hung up. Only then did he remember: "Oh, no—my passport! It's at the Indonesian Embassy!"

He phoned Bert's room. "Get over to the Indonesian Embassy as fast as you can," he ordered. "Pound on the door if you have to. Get my passport and meet me at the JUSMAG. Be there in twenty minutes, not a second later."

Larry went to the JUSMAG offices, signed in, and finally boarded the bus that would take him to the airport—still watching for Bert. The bus was slowly pulling away when a taxi slid to a stop. Bert popped out and ran alongside the bus. Larry calmly reached out the window, grabbed the precious document, and saluted.

"All set!" he told the driver.

Another problem: At the airport it was discovered that Larry's smallpox shots had expired. Quickly Captain William Robie of the U.S. military clinic at the airport prepared a syringe, gave him the vaccination, and signed the yellow chart. With a contingent of newsmen Larry hurried on board the C-46, whose engines were now running. It spun, aimed itself at the runway, lifted off, and set its course for Saigon.

As the plane began its descent for Tan Son Nhut Airport, the passengers could see the flares and the tracer bullets of war arching into the sky; but the plane landed safely. The passengers were told they would not be allowed to go into Saigon that night. They were taken to the officers' club where everyone found accommodations.

When Larry reached the World Vision office the following morning, the horror of the battle that had ringed the office with death was on everybody's lips. Big Mel Van Peursem had watched the fighting from a window, despite the danger. Early in the morning he had gotten into the World Vision Landrover and cruised the streets, picking up bullet-ridden Vietnamese and carrying them to the hospital.

"Big Mel was an absolute hero," Larry recalled. *"Time* magazine carried a special item telling about some of his activities. Later it was my very special privilege in the U.S. to present to him, at the request of the government of Vietnam, a medal that they awarded to Mel in gratitude for all he had done during the TET crisis, even at the risk of his own life."

Getting from Saigon to Surabaya, Indonesia, again required the logistics of divine synergism. Larry kept praying, working, and watching. He knew commercial air service still had not been resumed in or out of Saigon, but he felt that somehow he should go out to the airport and try.

"There are no civilian flights out of Saigon," he was told at Tan Son Nhut, but he was due in Singapore that night. Larry glanced out the window.

"What about that new Air Vietnam 727 sitting out there on the runway?" he inquired.

"Well, Air Vietnam has just taken delivery of it but it can't stay here. They're taking it to Singapore."

"Singapore! When?"

"Today. Very soon."

"Can I go along?"

"If you have a ticket."

"Sell me one!"

Larry was the only passenger on board that plane on the short flight to Singapore. He had only the clothes on his back, a few U.S. dollars, and a credit card. In Singapore he checked into the Goodwood Park Hotel, bought an extra shirt, some underwear, a toothbrush, and some shaving cream. A morning flight took him to Surabaya. Business finished there, he hired a taxi for $35 to carry him on the tedious, twenty-hour overland, dusty, hot journey through East Java back to Djakarta, where he would catch a return flight to Saigon. But just as he arrived at the airport he saw his plane taking off.

He checked his pockets: ten cents. He tried to find a hotel with an extra room but there was none. No place to go. No money for food. Suddenly the whole situation struck him as quite funny. Inside he had "this incredible feeling of peace. I was absolutely delighted to be on an adventure for God. I knew he was going to do something. Corrie ten Boom would have called it 'material for a miracle.'"

Suddenly a stranger approached. "Pardon me, but aren't you Larry Ward? Are you having some problem? I'm a pastor here in town and I recognized you from a World Vision pastors' conference which I attended."

They shook hands vigorously.

"Where are you staying?" the pastor asked.

"Well, that's my problem," Larry ventured.

"No problem. You come and stay at our house."

At supper, the pastor introduced Larry to tremendous needs in Borneo—the first of a chain of events which would lead to World Vision's involvement in direct aid. Larry began to think, "Now I know why I missed that plane!" But there was more.

When the meal was finished the pastor answered a knock at the front door.

"Dr. Ward, please come here a minute," the pastor called from the door.

When the caller saw Larry his mouth dropped open and he couldn't speak for a moment. "Larry Ward—I've been looking for you!" the young man cried. The son of David Morken, he had been dispatched to find Larry in connection with a projected series of World Vision-sponsored meetings. He had looked for Larry nonstop since arriving in Djakarta and was at the pastor's door only because the man he was with had stopped on another matter.

God works in answer to prayer.

Ho Chi Minh died the following year, and in 1970 the Indochina War became mired in even greater complexity. As in Larry's Civil War novel, *Thy Brother's Blood*, brother battled brother, and the South became no match for the ferocity and relentless determination of the forces from the North.

T. S. Eliot's poem, "The Waste Land," called April "the

cruelest month, breeding lilacs out of the dead land, mixing memory and desire, stirring dull roots and spring rain. . . ."

For South Vietnam it was the cruelest month indeed. Larry's *Living Light* for April 26, 1975, promised: "He is beloved of God and lives in safety beside him. God surrounds him with his loving care, and preserves him from every harm. Let him have all your worries and cares, for he is always thinking about you and watching everything that concerns you."

He would need it all. Streaming to the coastal cities in the sad "Convoy of Tears" came thousands of Vietnamese whose villages had been plundered. As a rescue plane in Nha Trang reached its capacity, throngs of people pressed in, desperate for a chance to escape. Somehow the door was forced shut, but people clung to the outside. The plane took off with refugees still holding onto the wings and wheels. When it landed in Saigon, the feet of dead Vietnamese could be seen hanging out of the wheelwells where they had sought to hide. They had been crushed to death when the plane stowed its landing gear on takeoff.

Amid the fiercest battles of the war, Larry continued his mission of service throughout South Vietnam. The village mentioned in the opening chapter of this book was Hiep Duc, on the morning after the Viet Cong had killed the district chief and his twelve-year-old daughter, leaving them hung on stakes. A small reconnaissance plane had spotted the grisly scene where 5,000 people had lost their homes in a burning inferno. Near the doorway of the command post, with the racket of war on all sides, Larry had looked down in the mud and found a Vietnamese New Testament opened to *Mac 16* (Mark 16), titled *Chua Jesus Song Lai* ("Jesus Christ Rises from the Dead"). In the midst of war, some brother or sister in Christ had been reminded by the Scriptures that "he that believeth in me, though he were dead, yet shall he live."

The end of the Indochina war was near, but what was surely Larry Ward's greatest experience of service lay ahead.

seventeen
THE THREE

Through the years, Larry has carried one special, deeply personal concern for Vietnam. It began over twenty years ago.

The dark night of May 30, 1962, lay humid and still on the sleepy jungle town of Banmethuot, Vietnam. Suddenly a cadre of barefoot Viet Cong soldiers shattered the stillness with machine-gunfire. They raced to the Christian and Missionary Alliance's leprosarium compound, tore open the doors, and ordered three missionaries to walk outside with their hands up. They rammed guns into their backs and led Dr. Eleanor Ardel Vietti, Archie Mitchell, and Mennonite volunteer Dan Gerber into the jungle, never to be seen since. The American people abruptly were made to realize North Vietnam's designs on the South.

Larry had visited Banmethuot on his first global journey and had formed a brief but close tie of friendship with Dr. Vietti. Had the Viet Cong needed medical help for fighting troops? Was it a new wave of violence against foreigners? Was it a signal that all Christians were in danger? Shock waves reverberated around the world. The Viet Cong, until this date, had advanced little more than threats.

The years of the Indo-China war ground on. The Christian church around the world prayed for the three missionaries' release. The hope of fellow believers, and later their resignation, was summed up by Archie Mitchell's thirteen-year-old daughter, Loretta, some three years after the kidnapping:

> In everything give thanks. The Lord knows we all love Daddy, but he wants Daddy for his work right now. Yes, "in everything give thanks." The only thing to do now is to stay and wait for the day when God's work through Daddy is finished, and then God will give Daddy back to us to enjoy.

Burning in Larry Ward's heart was a quiet determination to pursue relentlessly every possibility for finding "the three" as he always refers to these early MIAs. He traveled in and out of Vietnam seventy-seven times during his years as Vice President/Overseas Director of World Vision and later as President of Food for the Hungry. With every visit he carried the hope that this time he would stumble onto some clue which would lead to a resolution of this unfinished business and the release of these servants of Christ.

This hope led him time after time into the Central Highlands of Vietnam, where he suspected the missionaries and other U.S. prisoners of war might be held. Often a visit would yield some little clue which he added to the rest, careful to keep a guarded silence about what was happening, out of concern for the families of the American missing.

The war ground on for thirteen more years. American families gave 56,000 of their sons in the vain attempt to hold back the North.

The American combat forces had been withdrawn in 1972, yielding (in Larry's opinion) to at-home protests and media pressures rather than military reverses. American POWs in North Vietnam had been released in "Operation Homecoming," in January 1973. But Larry's friends—such as "the three" and Floyd Olson—were not among them.

With the direct American military presence withdrawn, the powerful forces from the North continued their war against the South, relentlessly pushing toward Saigon.

What about those missing missionaries and other Americans? Was there one last chance to get them out?

In November 1974, a tantalizing clue came from the Central Highlands where they had been captured. "Come and see," some Montagnard contacts told Larry. "We have access to Americans still held in Vietnam."

Larry was skeptical. He knew it had been almost two full years since the American POWs held in North Vietnam had returned via "Operation Homecoming." He was also well aware of the long-standing desire for autonomy on the part of the Montagnards (the mountain tribespeople living in the Central Highlands of Vietnam as a sometimes despised ethnic minority). He told his friend, "If this is some ruse to get guns and money, forget it. It's just too late in history."

But the quiet insistence was, "They want you to come and see for yourself. But first they want you to carry this news to your President."

So Larry went to the President of the United States—or at least as close as he could get. President Ford was then in Japan, but through the help of one of Larry's closest friends—Winston Weaver, a World Vision board member and Mennonite church leader from Harrisonburg, Virginia—he secured an immediate appointment with John O. Marsh, then Chief of Staff in the White House (and now the Secretary of the Army).

After a brief but encouraging conference with Mr. Marsh, whose courtesy Larry remembers with the deepest appreciation, there was a busy whir of meetings in the White House. Larry was assigned Dr. Ted Marrs (actually General Marrs, a retired Air Force medical leader) to be his principal contact.

It should be explained that even today certain elements of this story must be kept secret, for the safety of people remaining in Vietnam. Essentially, this situation in Vietnam had developed out of the zeal of Christian Montagnards in

South Vietnam in sharing the gospel with their fellow tribespeople who were serving on the side of the North. Warm ties of friendship had developed; the idea of "why do we fight other people's wars; why don't we get together?" had prevailed—and a special alliance had developed. This group, which was seeking American support, realized that one of the best ways to get this was to be able to prove the existence of Americans still missing in action in their Highlands.

The events of the months that followed—from November 1974, until late April 1975—could well be the subject of another book. It has been suggested that they would make the ingredients of an outstanding and successful Hollywood movie or TV presentation. They read like fiction, but they are all true. (Larry would add, "Sadly true.")

In the weeks that followed the November contact, Larry made several trips to Vietnam. He was there almost constantly from late January until the dying days of South Vietnam in late April.

High up in the hills of Central Vietnam he met with his Montagnard friends, and with their contacts from among what they called "the tribes in the jungle"—those who had been recruited by the Viet Cong or North Vietnam.

Larry remembers the unusual experience of personally typing a document ("poignantly historic," he calls it) which set forth the hopes of Montagnards. It was a unique "Declaration of Peace." It was their hope that their friend Larry Ward might read this for them on the floor of the United Nations, or arrange for some world leader to do so.

"It was interesting," recalls Larry, "how this developed. They were talking in a polyglot of tribal languages, Vietnamese, French, and—for my benefit—such English as they could muster. Then there would be a slow, laborious translation from one tribal language into another, and then into English for me . . . and then I would type it."

Larry still has a copy of that document. It says in effect that the tribespeople were tired of fighting someone else's war. They were ready to lay down their arms, except in defense of their own homes and families. It was especially meaningful to Larry because the whole basis of communication between these groups had been the sharing of the message of Jesus Christ. Now, as brothers in him, they were trying to unite . . . and were pleading to the outside world to help them.

Part of the plan was for Larry to visit the battle areas near Banmethuot to see at least a few of the American prisoners, and to receive evidence of others. But there were problems.

The original high-ranking officer he was to meet (who had become a Christian and was open to this contact) was recalled to Hanoi. Another man took his place—and for some weeks it was uncertain as to whether or not this new man could be trusted.

But finallly, on March 6, 1975—Larry was handed a cryptic note in Saigon. It said simply, "The Committee accepts the presence of the foreigner on the Committee. April 1."

This meant that at long last he was to meet with these people in the jungle and—if they did exist—to see some of the captured Americans. His heart beat fast as he boarded a flight for the United States. He stopped briefly at home, and then flew quickly across the United States to meet in the Pentagon with Dr. Robert Shields in the Department of Defense—the man who had coordinated Operation Homecoming and was now in charge of the continuing search for the American missing.

But hardly had Larry arrived in Washington when a telephone call from Saigon brought startling news. Banmethuot had fallen. Within a few hours this was followed by the announcement that President Thieu had withdrawn all his troops from the hills.

Larry's mission seemed doomed to failure. His rendezvous would be off, for there was apparently no way to keep that meeting in the jungle.

But back to Saigon he went, arriving one night and immediately flying the next morning to Dalat. It was a strange experience for Larry, for he and his young Montagnard friend, Ha Johnny (son of the famed Sao A) were the only passengers on the plane going into Dalat. The exodus was on, and everyone else was headed south while these two flew north on their mission of mercy.

"The next few days in Dalat were strange," summarizes Larry. "The missionaries had all fled, in response to a warning they had received that the Viet Cong or North Vietnamese were on their way. They can be forgiven for their sudden flight, for they knew that a number of their fellow missionaries had been captured in Banmethuot."

In Dalat, Larry and Johnny's brother Ha Jimmy had a long series of meetings with "a motley group" of tribal leaders.

The developments in the Highlands had produced some strange bedfellows. While Larry and the others met inside, Montagnard Viet Cong troops provided security outside.

A prime question in these discussions was how Larry as an American could make his way over the mountains into Banmethuot, to keep that long-postponed meeting. He would have been willing to try the long hike, but to do so would have endangered his companions. He was the last American left in the Highlands to anyone's knowledge, and there was no way he could have disguised himself effectively.

Finally a plan was established. If Larry and Ha Jimmy could fly over a rendezvous point in the jungles—the old "Camp Zulu" Special Forces Camp—friendly tribespeople on the ground would radio to them whether or not it was safe for them to fly ahead and land in Banmethuot, even though it was in Communist hands.

The problem was to get that plane.

Through a miraculous circumstance (described elsewhere in the book), Larry was able to fly with Jimmy south to Saigon on what was probably the last flight to leave Dalat. The city fell that night, as one of the "dominoes" toppling across central and northern South Vietnam.

Back in Saigon, Larry resolutely set out in search of that airplane. Dr. Marrs in the White House had given him the name of Colonel John Madison of the Joint Four-Party Military Team—the man who was in communication with the North Vietnamese and Laotian authorities about the American missing and other humanitarian issues.

"We need a light plane," Larry explained to Colonel Madison as he summarized the plan, "to fly over the Highlands. The Montagnards will be on the ground with a radio at 'Camp Zulu' in the Highlands and we will receive instructions from them as to whether or not we can land at Banmethuot."

Colonel Madison leaned back in his chair and reflected. He seemed helpful, but there was no hope in his speech. "Can you get to the Vietnamese?" he suggested.

Of course Larry could get to the Vietnamese, but he felt the American was missing the point. This new movement, the United Montagnard Front (UMF), would be a move against *all* Vietnamese. Their "wall of peace" would be a barrier against the Vietnamese of both North and South. Five months earlier the Montagnard who had carried this message to Saigon had disappeared and was believed to be dead. Larry's Montagnard friends were convinced that U.S. Embassy personnel had thoughtlessly relayed the Montagnards' report to the South Vietnamese, not understanding or thinking through all of the implications. They were almost certain that the South Vietnamese had "done him in."

Despite all that had happened, Larry now had no choice but to take his plea to the South Vietnamese. They might, he reasoned, see the UMF as an ally and at this late hour enter into the mission to keep their country free.

All this was taking place at a time when missionaries in other countries were suspected of being agents of the U.S. Central Intelligence Agency. Was Larry?

"I am not employed by the CIA, and never was. While I am not a pacifist—and while I still feel there are causes (such

as freedom) worth fighting for and dying for—I long ago
have learned as a Christian to hate war. My work has taken
me into just too many battlefields; my hands have been
stained with dying blood too many times. War cannot be
God's first choice for the people of his creation."

But now there was no choice. With the possibility that the
lives of Americans missing in action were at stake, he was
prepared to go to the Vietnamese with his plea. If they didn't
care about the missing Americans at least they might be interested in the potential military resource of some 200,000
united Montagnards—ready and probably able to retake
Banmethuot and Pleiku and Dalat. Even at this late date
they might feel there was a chance to reverse the "domino"
movement South Vietnam was experiencing. Lives were at
stake. Haste was important. To the Vietnamese he would go.

As he walked out of Colonel Madison's office he noticed
that the halls of the DAO were lined with boxes packed for
shipment home. One box in particular caught Larry's eye. It
was addressed to Col. John Madison, at an address in Ar-
lington, Virginia. "Colonel Madison was a good man,"
Larry relfects now. "But the total mentality in those hours
was exodus." Evacuation was in the air. What chance was
there to carry out his plan?

Larry went to colonels and generals and cabinet officials
of the South Vietnamese, contacting this person and that,
working his way up to General Cao Hao Hun in the office of
the Prime Minister . . . to his friend General Le Nguyen
Khang, Deputy Chief of the Joint Chiefs of Staff . . . to
many others of high rank.

What happened? The following is a typical reaction. For
over a half hour Larry poured out his heart to a high official . . . laid on him the whole story of the missing
Americans and the uniting Montagnards . . . presented his
need for just one little airplane to make a single pass over the
jungle.

The official listened intently. Larry knew this particular
Vietnamese spoke good English and had understood every

word. He leaned forward, waiting for helpful suggestions which he hoped would come from the man's expertise and authority. Instead the officer said earnestly, "My wife and I want to get out of here. Can you help us?"

Larry mumbled something and quickly left. Of course he would help the man if he could, but all in good time. At this time all he could think of was that haunting refrain: "We have seventy to eighty Americans . . . " and among them possibly "The Three" for whom the world of Christendom had prayed and for whom he had searched so long.

He had stood up for Howard Newton at Norwich High when a teacher had made a fool out of his classmate; now he would stand up for those in 1975 who could not rescue themselves.

From all of his meetings came one noteworthy contact. His good friend General Nguyen Van Chuc, now Deputy Minister for Refugee Resettlement, suggested that Larry meet with President Nguyen Van Thieu.

To Larry the thought "had of course occurred," because he had known the President since 1965 when Thieu was Chief of State. He had met with him a number of times at the palace and had been a dinner guest in Thieu's home. "But I knew that getting to him now would not be easy. Other high-ranking people who had proposed that I see the President had told me frankly that they didn't know how it could be arranged."

By now it was April 20, 1975. The friends in the jungle waited. President Thieu remained absolutely inaccessible, blockaded by his own staff for reasons still not clear. Larry needed an excuse to enter the palace and make his plea to the President.

But then Larry's old friend Bob Pierce arrived in Saigon, and he had his answer. Bob would be his "ticket." The plan would be to arrange an appointment for Bob with Madame Thieu, the President's wife. Ordinarily Larry would have called her to make an appointment for himself, but he had just met with her a few days earlier to discuss a joint refugee relief project with her ladies' committee. He needed a fresh excuse.

"Bob," Larry told his friend, "you are that excuse. All I want to do is to get inside the palace and tell Madame Thieu that I *must* see her husband."

The meeting was memorable. When Madame Thieu warmly welcomed them, Dr. Pierce came quickly to the point: "Madame Thieu," he said, "you know I'm glad to see you. But that's not why we are here. Larry *must* see your husband. It is a matter of the utmost importance."

Instantly she was on her feet. "I'll go get him."

Larry stood quickly, pleased but a bit startled. "We didn't mean *now,*" he said apologetically. "We thought perhaps you could make an appointment. . . ."

Madame Thieu shook her head. "I'll go get him," she said rather firmly, and quickly left the room.

A moment later the President himself appeared in the doorway. Without a word Madame Thieu and the ladies of her committee left the room before Larry could thank her.

For the next forty-five minutes, while Bob Pierce sat nearby praying silently, Larry poured out his story, starting from the beginning.

"Mr. President," he concluded, "you know that all these years we have never asked you for anything. We have just come, so many times, to offer our help. But this time, without apology, I *ask* you for something. I need an airplane. I need to fly over the jungles, to make the contact I have just told you about.

"Perhaps I have no reason to ask you to care about American lives at this point. I know you are bitter about the withdrawal of American support. I can understand your attitude. But on behalf of the parents in America who gave 56,000 of their sons to die for this country—and on behalf of the parents whose sons are still missing in action, for their sakes and out of respect for their sacrifice—I *plead* with you now to help me."

Larry had fought to hold his emotions in check as he

talked. Now it wasn't easy, for the President's own luminous eyes were suddenly wet with tears.

"I do not ask you, sir," Larry pressed on, "to risk any Vietnamese lives. All I need is an airplane. We will fly it ourselves. If you can't give me one, please sell me one. If I can't buy one, I may *steal* one. I *must* fly over the spot . . . I *must,* sir. Before I die I must know if any of this is true . . . if in fact there *are* American prisoners still alive out there."

President Thieu looked straight at Larry, his eyes now full of tears.

"Mr. President, there was a day in our country when the youth of America wore black armbands to protest the war. I understood their questions and confusion—but you may remember the cable I sent you on that day. It said, 'When the last American has left Vietnam, I will gladly come back and stand beside you and die with you, because of my great love for Vietnam.'"

Larry was too moved to say more, except one choked word. "Please."

Nguyen Van Thieu leaned back, holding out his hands, palms up. "What have we to lose?" he said, smiling now through his own tears. "What have we to lose?"

Suddenly Larry was aware of a presence in the doorway, even though he kept his eyes glued to the President's face. Thieu looked at his watch, then jumped to his feet. "Oh, I am late for a meeting," he said. "I am late. I will call you."

For the first time Bob Pierce spoke. "Mr. President," he said, in a strangely soft and gentle voice, "Larry and I would like to pray for you."

"Of course," said the President, "of course."

While the dignitaries waited in the next room for their meeting (apparently the one at which President Thieu would be "persuaded" to resign), three men stood close together in the palace and bowed their heads. The President reached out to put one arm around Larry, the other around Bob Pierce, as Bob prayed simply and to the point: "Father, help this man to do what is best for his country—whatever it costs him personally. In Jesus' name, Amen."

And the President softly echoed, "Amen."

Larry turned to the President, who took his right hand in both of his. With a face wet with tears he opened his mouth as if to speak, then bit his lip and shook his head, too full for words. He turned and left the room.

Several hours passed before Larry saw him again. As he entered the hotel where he was staying, Larry saw the President on television, announcing his resignation, bitterly lamenting the failure of the Americans to help South Vietnam in this, its last crisis hour of need.

Larry listened, sagged, and then went to his room and knelt beside his bed: "Father, I really don't understand this. I thought you had led me into all this. The President seemed to be our last hope, and. . . ."

But God's synchrony was right on time. Another drum was rolling in the distance. He had miles to go before he slept.

eighteen
LET MY PEOPLE GO!

It seems that all of Larry Ward's life has been an example of God's synchrony—the smooth blending of events to accomplish the Lord's purposes.

Nowhere has this been more evident than in those incredible last days in South Vietnam, in 1975.

To highlight just a few of the incredible concomitants that fitted into what Larry unhesitatingly describes as "the greatest experience of all my life," consider these three scenes and what they later represented.

Scene No. 1:
Larry sits on the Vietnam Airlines plane with his papers spread out before him, as usual making his airplane seat his "office." But now the papers lie untouched, as he talks with an earnest young Vietnamese flight steward. It is March 6, 1975—and the dominoes have not yet begun to fall in Vietnam. But this young flight attendant is something of a prophet. He is earnestly predicting to Larry that the fall of South Vietnam is not too long in the distance. By the time the flight has landed in Hong Kong, all that Larry can do is gather up his papers with a strange sense of God's leading. "I didn't get my work done, but somehow my heart tells me that there

was something very important about this contact. Perhaps in God's own time I will see what it was."

Scene No. 2:
Later that same day, on the continuing flight from Tokyo to the United States, Larry has unexpectedly encountered his old Vietnamese associate, Dr. Garth Hunt. Now Director of Living Bibles International in Canada, Garth listens with great interest as Larry reports the continuing chain of events in Vietnam. He and his associates, Dr. Jacob Bellig and Dr. W. Brooks, ply Larry with questions. When the flight lands, Larry deplanes with that strange and lingering sense of special significance related to this conversation.

Scene No. 3:
Flying this time *into* Vietnam, Larry is in an interesting conversation with a somewhat mysterious U.S. government person. The man holds (or at least had held) the rank of captain, he tells Larry; but he is nonspecific about his responsibilities. The two develop a quick rapport, and Larry enjoys the conversation—and yet, again, his heart somehow tells him that the significance of the conversation lies beyond that day.

Why these scenes? What do they represent? Consider these developments:

Scene No. 1 Flashback:
It is over a month later. Larry and his companion Ha Jimmy find themselves in a scene of incredible confusion—"almost chaos"—in the airport in Dalat, high up in the Central Highlands of Vietnam. To Larry's knowledge, he is the last American in those hills. The rush is on, the wild flight to the South. Larry and Ha Jimmy *must* get to Saigon. There are important developments related to his long-standing concerns about those American MIAs. But there are no seats on the plane . . . and the wild crowd, jostling and almost

fighting for seats, waving fistfuls of U.S. dollars, doesn't even permit him to reach the counter. Being an American, at this late date in Vietnam's history, is of no advantage. Suddenly Larry feels a hand on his arm. He turns—and here is that same steward whom he had met on the flight from Saigon to Hong Kong.

"Some problem?"

Larry nods. "I need two seats to Saigon."

"Don't talk," the steward says crisply. "Meet me inside." Inside he hands Larry two tickets . . . and within a matter of minutes Larry and Jimmy are airborne, headed for Dalat. *What they do not know is that that night Dalat will fall.* On board the plane, Larry chats with the steward. "I know you understand, sir," the young man says, "why I couldn't talk with you in there. Everyone wants to get out."

"Of course," Larry replies. "Do you come to Dalat often?"

The steward looks at him strangely. "You remember me. I met you on the flight from Saigon to Hong Kong. I am an *international* steward. This is *the only time in my life* I ever come to Dalat!"

Looking back on that scene, Larry says: "Humanly speaking, I owe my life to that young man. He was in exactly the right spot at the right time to help Jimmy and me—and I know God had his hand in this."

Scene No. 2 Flashback:

April 25, 1975. Larry once again is in a scene of noise and confusion, at the Tan Son Nhut Airport. This is the U.S. military's command center for organizing the escape from Vietnam for people who must get out. With Larry are a small group of friends (the vanguard of the many hundreds he is to help in the next few hours). They *must* get out of Vietnam. These are people who have distinguished themselves in the service of their country. They have had links with the U.S. government, just by virtue of that country's presence in their land.

Larry looks around uncertainly; he doesn't know just how

to start or what to do. Suddenly he looks across the room. Standing there is Dr. Garth Hunt.

Larry has often said, "One of the greatest tributes I could pay to Garth Hunt is that somehow I was not the least bit surprised to see him there in Vietnam. He had been away for over three years. He had no reason to be there. I found out later that he had promised his wife Betty as he left for Asia that this is one place he would not go, back into the dangers of Vietnam."

But Garth Hunt's heart—the constraining love of Christ— had drawn him back to that country where he and Betty had served so long and faithfully. Friends of his were in trouble, and he was determined to help. Also, he knew that there in Saigon was the unfinished manuscript to the new Vietnamese New Testament—the first such translation in readable language that the Vietnamese people had had for many years. He was determined to get that manuscript and bring it out, along with any of his friends he could help. But, as a Canadian, it would be very difficult for him to sponsor anyone in the midst of this frantic exodus.

Now there is a quick look of recognition on his part, and then the two quietly go to work.

Garth has been there long enough to size up the situation. He directs Larry to the desks in the command center where U.S. civilians are presenting their case for Vietnamese friends they want to help out of the country.

Scene No. 3 Flashback:
Larry shrugs, selects one of the lines at random—and then looks in astonishment at the man behind the desk. It is that same mysterious person with whom he had flown into Saigon. There is a flicker of recognition, but no direct communication. Larry understands, and when his turn comes, quietly steps up to represent his case.

The man tells him what to do and hands him the necessary forms. As Larry walks away, he realizes that in those papers he now has the key which can unlock the door to freedom for unknown numbers of his friends.

A moment later he sees the man behind the desk enjoying a cup of coffee during a little break. Larry slips over beside him. "I know you understand why I couldn't especially greet you," the man says. "Everybody has a case to present here."

Larry assures him he understands—and then asks, "Is this the procedure we follow? I have many others I want to help."

Assured that it is, he breathes a word of thanks and walks on . . . into the middle of one of life's greatest service experiences. All told, he and Garth are to help over 1,800 people find a new life of freedom in other parts of the world.

"THESE TWO MEN CRIED . . . "
Together Garth and Larry went to work. In addition to those who were now already on their way to the United States or elsewhere abroad through their efforts and Larry's specific sponsorship, there were many others to be helped.

In the hours that followed they fanned out all over the city, contacting these people, going again and again to the airport. One of Garth's contacts was with a beloved friend who for years had been the leader of the Protestant Evangelical Church in Vietnam. "Sir," Garth pleaded, "you must come with me. You have been in America; you have been known as the friend of the Americans—at least the American missionaries. Please come."

The servant of God smiled gently. "Thank you, Mr. Hunt—but as the president of the church I am like the captain of the ship. I should be the *last* to leave. Not all of our pastors will be able to go. I'm grateful for those you can help, but I will stay. Just pray for me . . . that I do not fail my test."

As the hours went by, it became increasingly difficult to

reenter the airport. Larry and Garth never knew for certain whether they themselves would be permitted through the gates—or if they would be able to bring any more of their Vietnamese friends in.

They had, however, an important residue of about seventy key people whom they had asked to meet them on a certain corner in the city of Saigon. The big question was to figure out how to get them in—past the Vietnamese guards and then past the American guards and on board the planes that would carry them to safety.

Probably not even realizing the unusual importance of what they were doing, the two agreed to charter a city bus. Loaded with its precious cargo of men and women, boys and girls, it approached the gates of Tan Son Nhut Airport.

It must have presented an odd spectacle. Here were the many jeeps, the chauffeur-driven Mercedes cars—all being turned away at the gates.

And then here came this gaudy city bus. Leaning out of one window was Garth Hunt, barking away in his fluent Vietnamese.

Leaning out of the other side was Larry Ward, waving a sheaf of papers that bore the red corporate seal of Food for the Hungry/Vietnam.

Up ahead was a car driven by an American working with the USAID program. He was holding a radio in his hand, periodically talking into the radio and then pointing back over his shoulders to the bus behind.

Larry, meanwhile, was holding a similar small radio, and pointing earnestly at the white car which was preceding them.

No matter that both of those radios were dead. They were all part of a very convincing, confusing, and therefore effective approach.

The guards could handle those generals in the jeeps and those big Mercedes cars. They just didn't know what to do with the bus—or with these two foreigners talking all at once in a mixture of rapid-fire Vietnamese and English. The gates rolled open—and the bus entered.

The events which followed could easily fill a book or make a movie.

They were miracles of God's timing.

Larry had gone so many times to the desks to present his case that finally someone handed him a whole sheaf of airplane manifest forms. "No point in duplicating our work, mister," someone said. "Just fill these out and bring them in."

In Larry's hands, therefore, were the papers that could bring hundreds—literally thousands—of Vietnamese outside. And he had that many whom he knew personally. He would unhesitatingly vouch for them, and without hesitation sign his name to the paper assuming all responsibilities for their future conduct in the United States.

Time and again one of those sheets of paper would have a certain number of spaces to be filled out. For example, there might be five spaces—and just at that moment a mother and father would appear with their three young children.

By the time that Larry and Garth themselves finally boarded the flight that was to carry their last group on its way, every single person with whom they had been able to establish direct contact had been put on those manifests. The lists had come out "exactly right."

There was a scene at the gate that Larry will never forget. Assisting him and Garth was a remarkable lady, Madam Nguyen Ngoc Le. President of the Vietnam War Widows Association, widow of a famous general, former head of the Vietnamese Red Cross, she had been one of the most outstanding Vietnamese in helping her people through the years.

Today she herself was a general. As Garth and Larry brought their various groups up to the actual place where they would go through the final gate to board the planes, she was there—barking out orders in Vietnamese. "Stand straight," she would say. "Be proud. Leave your country with your head high."

But finally when Garth had led the last group through the gate and only Madam Le and her friend Larry remained, she looked at him—and wilted. Placing her head on his shoulder, she sobbed over and over again: "Now those terrible men will destroy my beautiful country. Now those terrible men will destroy my beautiful country!"

It was as if she herself, in leaving, somehow felt that this was the ultimate surrender. Larry placed a gentle arm around her shoulders and supported her as they boarded and then—with the rest of the refugees—sat down on the floor of the plane to be lifted from the scenes of confusion below.

What they did not know was that that very night the airport would be rocketed and the first forces of the Viet Cong and the North Vietnamese would come spilling in. The flights would be suspended, and anyone else leaving would have to be evacuated by helicopter.

They flew to Clark Field in Manila—and what Larry insists on calling "the miracles" continued. For example, there were three groups about which he felt a special concern. The one that he and Garth had accompanied, and two others.

But they did not know where the other two were. Perhaps they had flown directly to Guam, or even to the United States.

Larry was anxious to keep his group together. Already, flying from Saigon to Manila, he and Garth had mapped out the concept that was going to result in the formation of "Hope Village" in the United States. He wasn't just going to dump all those Vietnamese on the American economy. He was going to set up a job placement and a general orientation program, to help them really succeed.

They had helped him, and others like him, in their own country. He was determined to help them.

But how and where would he go about finding those two groups in particular, and then the many others he had signed out of Vietnam?

The answer was not long in coming. Larry and Garth and their group had arrived late at night at Clark Field. The next morning, along with thousands of other refugees, they were being bussed to the processing centers on Clark Field.

As their bus neared one corner—a four-way stop—Larry shouted out. "Garth, look! There's one of our groups!"

Shouting to his driver to wait, Larry leaped out of the bus and raced into the center of the intersection waving frantically at the other bus. Out of that bus came one of his Vietnamese friends, and they fell into each other's arms. But suddenly they turned as they heard another shout. From another corner came a tall Vietnamese friend—the leader of the third group. He reached out and threw his arms around Larry in a big bear hug.

Providentially, those three groups had arrived at that very intersection at the exact same moment.

There was a quick conversation. "Where are you staying? What section?"

Arrangements were made—and within hours these three groups—and about 150 other people—were on the next leg of their journey toward Guam.

But at Andersen Field in Guam, it seemed that they had run into a snag. Larry had earnestly pleaded with the authorities to allow him to take his entire group to the United States together. He had that "Hope Village" concept in mind. With him were the 241 who had flown from Clark Field to Guam, and now others had joined their number—so he and Garth had about 360 or more in their custody.

The young lieutenant who was in charge of the program listened sympathetically, but finally shook his head. "Sorry," he said, "but I don't think I can help you. This is all computerized. There are no groups. The people just go by individual families, as their numbers are called."

Larry and his little band stepped aside and looked at each other. In Guam he and Garth had been joined by missionary John Newman, his old friend from Dalat, who had left Vietnam some weeks before the fall; Reverend John Sawin, veteran Christian and Missionary Alliance missionary; and Larry's good friend Drew Sawin, John's son.

"Let's call the White House," someone said. "Let's call Billy Graham!" (Drew had informed the group that he was aware that the White House was indeed monitoring the progress of this group around the world, and that he had been informed that Billy Graham was going to have breakfast with President Ford.)

Larry shook his head. "Guys," he said quietly, "the Lord himself has brought us this far. We have seen his miracles. Let's just trust him."

About fifteen minutes later that young lieutenant suddenly burst into their barracks. "Can you get your group together?"

Larry smiled. "They're all right here. We have already called them together."

"Well," the lieutenant said, "we don't understand it—but a 747 has just come in which somehow was missed on schedule. It's all yours if you want it! It will take your whole group, and a few more."

A few days later, as the refugees were being loaded into the buses which would carry them to their plane, Larry stepped over to thank the lieutenant. "Aw," the man insisted, "I was just doing my job."

"No," said Larry gratefully, "you have done more—and we'll be forever grateful."

The lieutenant looked at Larry for a long moment and then said quietly: "I was a prisoner in North Vietnam. I just had to help."

Larry has often said that it seemed that all along the line, God had the right people at the right place at the right moment to help. These were people whose hearts had been touched in some special way.

As they boarded the Pan Am jet, Garth and Larry stepped up to the helpful stewardess. "We would like to give some instructions to them, in Vietnamese—and then, if it's all right with you, we would like to have a special prayer." She readily agreed, and a moment later Garth's rapid-fire Vietnamese crackled over the plane sound system. Then he brought to the microphone an aged patriarch of the church, Pastor Le Van Thai, to lead in prayer.

"I will never forget that prayer," Larry recalls. "I can't have a dry eye as I recall those words. Pastor Le Van Thai not only thanked God for their deliverance, but prayed especially for the church left behind, for their brothers and sisters and friends, and for all of their country, in the hours of trial which would follow."

And then that big bird stretched what Larry always calls "its happy wings" and mounted into the sky.

As the plane flew along toward the United States, in the quiet of the night, Larry silently walked from one end to the other. His heart was full of praise to God. He looked down on his sleeping Vietnamese friends, many of whom he had known so well through the years. "I felt like the last chapter of a Grace Livingston Hill book," he says with a chuckle, "with all the characters assembled in the last chapter. Here they were, relaxed and happy—on their way to freedom."

And then, leaning back to relax, he remembered that night in early April when it had become apparent to him that the forces of the North were going to prevail. He thought of all of those with whom his life had been linked in service through the years. He remembered those who had been approaching him—everywhere he went—asking him if he could help them get out.

And, reflecting now on the airplane en route to the United States, he remembered that particular day when all of this had burdened his heart so that he had fallen on his knees in prayer in his hotel room. He had been praying for this one and that one, and for all of troubled Vietnam. Suddenly his prayer had reached such an intensity that he found himself on his feet, holding up his hands to God and crying out: "Let my people go!"

That had been his cry. He had cried . . . and the Lord had heard him.

nineteen
"PROJECT NOAH"

They called it "Project Noah"—and Larry Ward will always regard it as one of life's greatest experiences.

But he has to admit it came to a rather untimely and inglorious end.

"Project Noah" was one of the first efforts (very likely *the* first) of Vietnamese refugee "boat people" to escape from their war-shattered homeland.

This espisode itself could fill a book and make exciting grist for an adventure movie. It has an unusual cast of characters: the indefatigable Larry Ward, the peripatetic Dr. Bob Pierce, miscellaneous high-level Vietnamese (disguised as homeless refugees), a lovable old Navy salt named Bill Pride (whom Larry describes as "more by nature than most of us are by grace"), and a colorful and much-decorated Air Force hero, Colonel Jack Bailey (whom Larry simply and sincerely labels "the most genuinely compassionate person I have ever met").

The "scenes" rival the cast: secret meetings, code names (Larry's was "Gray Eagle"), a mysterious cache in Larry's hotel room (with smoke grenades, an unloaded machine gun, and even an American flag!)—and a wild chase through Saigon streets, with gunfire shattering the curfew quiet.

Try one sample episode: Larry's hotel room is jammed with Vietnamese (perhaps twenty or thirty) waiting for the signal to rush to the docks for their escape from Vietnam on two small ships. It had been decided that Larry should stay on to handle any problems which might arise with the Vietnamese government. Jack Bailey would accompany these first boat people, who would head for the Philippines as soon as they reached the open sea.

Bill Pride, the old Navy hand, had flown to Manila to make arrangements with the government there. Because these were the first of the boat people, no one knew how President Marcos might react. (Larry had planned Project Noah originally to help fourteen Vietnamese staff of the Far East Broadcasting Company in their escape from Vietnam, and so now he had sent Bill Pride to FEBC in Manila.)

Telephone and telegraph facilities were almost non-existent in these dying hours of South Vietnam. Anyway, this was a highly secret mission.

So Larry had devised a code. FEBC news broadcasts could be picked up in Saigon, and so he sent word via Bill Pride to Newscaster Carl Lawrence to give a coded message on the morning news.

Larry will never forget that day—and that electric moment when Carl flashed the word: "That concludes the news," he said, "and now here's a thought for the day. Take *pride* in your lawn. . . ."

That was the first signal! Bill Pride had made contact. But what would come next? If Carl continued, "make your neighbors *red* with envy," that would signal a delay, or a problem.

"Take pride in your lawn," stated Carl Lawrence in Manila. "Make your neighbors . . . *green* with envy!"

Larry leaped to his feet. "It's a *go*. Scramble!"

His group rushed out of the hotel, raced to waiting cars and hurried toward the docks. All over Saigon others switched off their radios—and scrambled.

The rest of the story will have to wait for another telling

(perhaps another book). Suffice it to say that Project Noah hit a premature Ararat—when the 132 refugees and Colonel Jack Bailey were stopped by crooked elements of the South Vietnamese police four hours down the Saigon River.

It was not a legal arrest. It was kidnap and ransom, with the entire party held for days in a dirty warehouse on the riverfront. When an angry Larry tracked them down, first of all demanding the release of the American, Bailey was rushed away in a jeep, perhaps to be disposed of. Knowing that Larry was running behind the jeep, Jack attempted to escape. That's when the shots rang out. Unfortunately, Jack leaped from the jeep in front of a jail, and was immediately captured and dragged inside.

For over a week Jack suffered in that jail, actually in a "dungeon underneath the jail," as he puts it. He was threatened, beaten, tortured—and even, he says, given truth serum in the attempt to find out who this mysterious Larry Ward was and where he could be located.

On the advice of high-level Vietnamese friends, Larry himself finally went into hiding—first in an empty apartment, and then in a hotel under an assumed name.

After a long week, Jack's release was finally obtained—by direct presidential order—after some of Larry's Vietnamese friends had intervened.

"Jack still bears both the physical and psychological scars of that ordeal," Larry summarizes. "But he has kept on helping, first in our 1975 Hope Village operation for Indochina refugees and later when he launched his own mercy ship operation in the South China Sea." Food for the Hungry donated its S.S. *Akuna* to Jack's program in 1982.

twenty
HIS BROTHERS' KEEPER

South Vietnam fell on April 30, 1975, ending a thirty-year carnage for the Vietnamese people and putting an end to the American nightmare which had taken the lives of 56,000 G.I.s. Larry's exodus from Vietnam (in which he was able to take with him some 1,800 people who might have been killed or imprisoned by the invaders) has been described in the preceding chapter.

"I am certain," he told his associates back in the United States, "that Vietnamese now are going to pour into Thailand by the thousands. Let's get in there and see what we can do right away to prepare for them."

That foresight allowed Food for the Hungry to be one of the first humanitarian agencies from outside to be ready with aid to these homeless people.

On his first tour of a camp in northern Thailand, Larry noticed a young Hmong tribesman following him as he inspected the facilities. His eyes were bright, his countenance sad. When he got the chance he whispered to Larry in perfect English, "Sir, it is true. We do have food and we do have place to sleep. But, sir, we have no hope."

"No hope." The words stung. The people had fled with nothing, but that is not what caused them the worst suffering. It was a lack of hope for the future. Before Larry stepped into the khaki-colored Thai government helicopter to leave, he looked up into the sky. "Lord," he prayed, "there is always hope with you. But what hope can you provide for these people?"

Sleep came hard that night because the face of the Hmong intruded and he heard over and over the words, "No hope."

The Hmong are ambitious and bright, but essentially Stone Age people. This young man who could speak English had probably worked in some capacity for the U.S. government.

The following day brought a call from Lionel Rosenblatt, chief of U.S. refugee operations in Thailand. (Larry describes Lionel as "a real hero in South Vietnam's last days, and an outstanding foreign service officer.") Rosenblatt had seen Food for the Hungry's Hope Village in California and now wanted to discuss with Larry some matters concerning the refugees in Thailand.

They met in the coffee shop of the Asia Hotel in Bangkok where Rosenblatt introduced Dr. Yang Dao, one of the educated exceptions among the basically illiterate Hmong refugees. He had earned a Ph.D. in France, had served as a high official in the government of Laos before leaving as a refugee, and was now concerned about the future of his people.

"Dr. Ward," he said in heavily accented English, "I know that you want to help my people. But please remember, we are a people in need of development. Please do not take us to your country or to Canada, or to France, or to Australia. We will not fit in."

Then he added a line which somehow made the light go on: "Somewhere in the world there must be a developing country where we can go and develop with it . . . and even contribute to its development."

Larry looked at Dr. Yang Dao and said, "Thank you." Then he looked straight up and breathed a quick prayer, "And thank *you*, God."

176

After the meeting he rushed back to his room. "Lorraine, Honey, we have a job to do," he said to his wife, rubbing his hands together vigorously, with his lips pinched tightly shut. "We've got to scour this earth. God has given us the formula for helping these people find a future and a hope. Not just to come to America where they really won't fit in, but to locate in some developing country which needs people like them."

The trail led first to the welcome arms of Nicaragua, where permission actually was obtained to bring in a pilot group of 15,000 Vietnamese refugees. But Larry and his associates quickly backed off when they sensed the human rights issues involved . . . and felt that the refugees would have been placed in a very dangerous situation.

But the experience of studying the situation in Nicaragua had led to a clear understanding of what could be accomplished by "resettlement through development" or, perhaps more correctly, "development through resettlement."

Larry states: "We are grateful for the learning experience of the negotiations with Nicaragua and the Somoza government. They had about 2 percent of their people living in 47 percent of their land mass in the Atlantic Zone. It could have been an ideal situation for the refugees—except that we could see the war clouds on the horizon. But we did grow all the more reinforced in our conviction that here was a solid answer to the refugee resettlement problem in the world. The secret would be to take people not just where they would be accepted on humanitarian grounds, but where they would be welcome because they were *needed.*"

There were other contacts—with Argentina and with Paraguay, for example, but here again concern for the refugees and their best interests seemed to indicate that these would not be the best situations.

And then came Bolivia, and for Larry Ward "one of the strangest experiences of all my life."

Bolivia was the ideal example of a country which needed people . . . and especially jungle farmers such as the refugees. In early 1978, arrangements were completed to bring in a pilot group of 100 families.

On the surface, it seemed ideal. Each family would receive 120 acres of land—free. They would have full citizenship rights after one year, upon application. And Food for the Hungry as the coordinating agency would be there to assure that their human rights were protected.

In April 1978, Larry signed the official agreement with the Ministry of Foreign Affairs of the government of Bolivia. This was done in the presence of two Hmong refugees who had been flown to Bolivia to survey the situation for themselves.

The refugees returned to their fellows in Thailand, like the two in the Bible who had gone to "spy out the land." They reported enthusiastically and affirmatively, and in a single day more than two thousand people signed up to go to Bolivia.

Food for the Hungry sprang into action. Spanish classes, with additional instruction concerning orientation to life in Bolivia, were begun in Thailand.

Back in Bolivia, land was cleared. Food and vehicles and a large tractor were rushed in.

But then, about three months after the signing of the agreement, there was a major political change in Bolivia. The events which followed in the succeeding several years "would have been funny, if so much had not been at stake," Larry recalls.

Again and again, as the government in Bolivia changed nine or ten times, word came to Larry Ward to come back to reopen contacts with the Bolivian government. Each time a new agreement was reached—only to fall by the way as that government was replaced by still another.

"Under any other circumstances, we would not have kept trying," Larry recalls. "But this seemed so ideal. We could combine two problems to get one solution. Bolivia had the problem of not enough people; Thailand had the problem of too many people. It seemed to be one of those rare situations in which everyone would win and no one would lose."

But it was not to be.

After several years of arduous effort, Food for the Hungry reluctantly had to lay the project aside.

Larry smiles ruefully as he talks about this complicated situation. "I trust God, and I cheerfully accept the fact that this just did not work out. But I sorta hope he will explain it all to me someday! You see, our main purpose in this was to show that God *always* has the answers. Just as he has the answers to the problems of individuals and families, he has the answers for men and nations—if they will just look to him.

"This, really, was our 'bottom line.' We felt that this project could be a great demonstration of how God could have an answer so simple and yet so profound that the world would overlook it."

But, overall, the effort wasn't wasted. Out of those first contacts in Bolivia on behalf of the refugees came very significant programs for the Bolivians themselves.

In 1978, Food for the Hungry began a series of feeding programs in Bolivia which in 1982 were extended to massive scale. Bolivia had been declared one of the neediest nations in all the world, and Food for the Hungry was there to help.

Millions of pounds of food were supplied by the U.S. government, and Food for the Hungry coordinated the gargantuan feeding effort. (This was the first time that Food for the Hungry had received any direct assistance from the American government, except for minor direct grants from U.S. Embassies overseas.)

And it all began with a refugee who cried out for help . . . and with Larry Ward, who in turn cried out to God on his behalf.

twenty-one
"GOD DID SEND A SHIP"

Following the major political change in Indochina in 1975, the world was suddenly awash with scurrying refugees, complicating disaster and famine conditions. The first refugees fled to the United States; then a huge wave of them moved westward to Thailand, while others set off into the dangerous waters of the South China Sea on dilapidated and precariously overloaded little barks. They drifted toward Malaysia, Hong Kong, the Philippines, and Singapore as well as Thailand.

In 1980, after Russian troops stormed into Afghanistan, hundreds of thousands of Afghan refugees fled into Pakistan. As fighting raged in the Ogaden, a disputed area between Ethiopia and Somalia, additional refugees were created. Somalia became the scene of one of the world's biggest refugee crises.

Into all these areas went Larry Ward with his mission of help. But always through the years his heart was especially haunted by the reports of the boat people. During the final days of South Vietnam's struggle he had had what he terms that "dubious distinction" of putting the first of the boat people into the water through "Project Noah."

Through 1976 and 1977 those little boats kept coming: First a trickle, then a giant wave. Why?

"I could not live under the Communists," many said. Others commented simply, over and over: "We wanted to be free." One summarized: "My family and I had to escape from the biggest prison in the world, which is Vietnam today." They would rather risk their lives on small boats and sail into raging waves and the threats of pirates than to remain in the country of their birth.

Larry and his associates found a former Australian naval vessel—a famous ship, the S.S. *Gladstone,* whose guns had shot down the first Japanese "Zero" attack plane in World War II. It had been decommissioned from the Australian Navy, and reregistered under an aboriginal name, the *Akuna.*

The stately old convoy ship was 190 feet long and weighed over 700 metric tons. Once its decks had known the feet of some of Australia's finest, defending their country. Now they were to feel the steps of as many as 100 to 150 Vietnamese "boat people" at a time—and sometimes to be washed by their grateful tears, after they had been rescued from the rugged waters of the South China Sea.

There was an apricot glow in the eastern sky that morning of the first launch in January 1979. Through the harbor waters of Singapore the S.S. *Akuna* churned northwesterly into the South China Sea, and then sailed north along the Indonesian coast. Thousands of Food for the Hungry donors had given small gifts to help; friends like Pat Robertson, Jerry Falwell, and Billy Graham had moved their organizations to help. The rescue mission was on its way.

Just before coming up on deck for the early morning watch that second day out of Singapore, Larry knelt in trusting prayer in his tiny cabin. Suddenly in his heart he felt "a mighty surge of joy. Somehow I knew, even before I climbed to the bridge, that this was it—the day we had long awaited! Contact!"

On board the ship that fateful day were a number of students from Dr. Falwell's Liberty Baptist College. One of them had been on watch, and now Larry was to relieve her.

As he climbed the ladder, she shook her head disconsolately. "We haven't seen anything yet," she said sadly.

Larry grinned. "Stick around! We are going to see one right now." He wasn't saying it jokingly or boastfully. God had put that confidence in his heart.

He picked up the binoculars and began to scan the horizon, back and forth, back and forth.

Almost immediately he saw it. A tiny boat. Dead ahead—"12 o'clock." Straining as if to extend the range of his binoculars, he could see on board what appeared to be several people. They were still, motionless, but easily discernible.

Without a word he handed the binoculars to the first mate and pointed. As the mate focused on the little boat, slowly coming into good binocular range, his eyes opened wide. "I theenk so!"

The distance shortened and still the people visible on the shallow, open boat remained silent and cautious. (Larry and his crew could not know at that hour of the cruel and inhuman piracy which had robbed the people of their food and belongings.) Quickly he huddled with his interpreter-chaplain Ha Jimmy, son of the famous tribal evangelist Sao A. Ha Jimmy raised his battery-operated megaphone. Across the water rang out words which almost every Vietnamese would know: *"Tin Lanh! Tin Lanh!"* ("Good News!") This would have a double meaning, for South Vietnam was dotted with little evangelical churches identified by the term *Tin Lanh*—"the 'good news' church."

Immediately the S.S. *Akuna* crew sensed the reaction. Suddenly many people were visible on the refugee boat. They had begun to move excitedly, to point, to wave.

Now, about a hundred yards away, they could hear Jimmy's full announcement in Vietnamese: "We are friends. We are Christians. We have come to help you! Do you need help? We have food, water, medicines. . . ."

By now the little boat was wildly alive. Everyone was waving excitedly. Some held up water cans, shaking them and pointing as if to show that they were empty.

"*Gom on!*" they cried. "*Gom on!*" ("Thank you! Thank you!")

"As long as I live, I shall remember the joy and excitement of those busy minutes which followed," Larry recalled. "We came alongside, threw down ropes, drew them closer, began to talk in a happy babble of mixed Vietnamese and English. There were eighty-eight on board, we found, and they had been six days at sea."

In the midst of the happy celebration, as the Liberty Baptist students and crew were handing out the bags of food and water and fresh fruit, Larry's attention was drawn to one woman in particular. Her head was bowed, her face in her hands.

Concerned, he called down to her, "Are you all right?"

As she slowly lifted her head, Larry could see that her face was wet with tears. She placed her hand over her heart, as if in an instinctive gesture, and replied in English: "Oh, I am 'Tin Lanh' too! I am Christian. Seven of us on board, we are Christians."

Minutes later, after the Liberty Baptist collegians and the crew of the S.S. *Akuna* had loaded them down with food and water and fruit and little stoves and fresh milk and vitamins, there was a quick prayer. And then the refugees were directed to a friendly shore where they could be helped in a refugee camp until there would be opportunity for resettlement in Canada or the United States or elsewhere.

As the little boat sailed away Larry turned to Ha Jimmy: "Just think, Jim, how those seven Christians will find their witness for Christ enhanced! Now they can remind the other eighty-one people that we helped them because we are Christians—because of the constraining love of our living Lord and Savior, Jesus Christ!"

For Larry Ward, that by itself would have been one of life's golden moments. But there was more to the story.

A few weeks after that memorable first mission, he was back in his home in Scottsdale, Arizona, when a letter arrived from California. It came from a young lady working with the great radio ministry of Far East Broadcasting Company. She wrote: "By God's grace my younger sister got out of Vietnam recently, and she was one of eighty-eight that you helped when they ran out of fuel, food, water." (She had seen her sister's picture in a Food for the Hungry report-advertisement in *Christianity Today,* and now a letter had come from the sister, in a refugee camp in Malaysia.)

She quoted from her sister's letter: "We were waiting to die. But we prayed—and *God did send a ship* to rescue us."

Larry was at home when he read those words. Without a word he headed straight for his bedroom and fell to his knees beside his bed. His heart was full of praise to God. It had been worth it all—all the effort and strain and struggle to raise the money for the ship. (He and Lorraine had actually mortgaged their home to provide the funds for the purchase of the ship.)

"Lord," he prayed gratefully, "life doesn't hold any greater privilege than this . . . to be part of your gracious answer to somebody's desperate prayer. Thank you, Lord, for allowing us to help."

On another day the S.S. *Akuna* arrived in Singapore with a boatload of tearfully grateful Vietnamese who had set out to sea on an inadequate boat. Hundreds of others had been rescued, but none more grateful than these. After Larry spoke to them through Ha Jimmy, one of the group stood up to reply:

"We wish we had something to give you," he said. "But we left everything behind in Vietnam—and what little we had was taken away from us by the pirates. But we do want you to have this. . . ."

And the refugee held out the compass which they had removed from their little boat before it sank.

Larry took the gift and bowed. He was full of emotion and found it difficult to speak.

"I feel like another pirate to take your compass," he finally said, smiling through his tears. "But you will not need it now, for you are safe here on the deck of our ship."

Then he added: "Ha Jimmy and I have just given you another and even more important Compass—the Bible, the Word of God. You will need this special Compass as you begin your new life in America or some other part of the world. There will be problems there—problems of adjustment, problems when people do not understand you.

"Follow this Compass, the Bible. Let it lead you straight to God. Just as your compass brought you to safety on our ship, so this Compass, the Bible, can lead you to the new life found only in God through belief in Jesus Christ, his only Son."

There was an interesting sequel to all of this, actually in two parts. Larry will never forget that Christian lady whom he met in the rugged waters of the South China Sea. After their dramatic encounter out there, he was not to see her again until he met her with Dr. Jerry Falwell before live television cameras in the United States. What a dramatic reunion! But there was more. He learned only then that her sister—who had written from the Far East Broadcasting Company to report her sister's safe arrival in Malaysia, and to quote her words of gratitude—had been one of the first fourteen people Larry had been asked to help back there in Saigon in 1975. She had been one of that original group for whom he launched "Project Noah," in April 1975!

twenty-two
THANK GOD FOR A SENSE OF HUMOR

Just in from Russia, Larry Ward hurried across a New York hotel lobby and jumped into an elevator just as its doors were closing. It was full of suitcases and people, so Larry had no room to turn around, but instead found himself pinned in, facing all the other passengers.

Somehow the people in the elevator seemed strangely silent to Larry, and they all seemed to be wearing similar expressions of shock. Then he remembered. Perched on his head was a Russian-looking fur cap (actually from Afghanistan, where he had purchased it en route to Moscow).

As the elevator continued its slow and silent ascent, it seemed to Larry that something (anything, really) should be said to ease the awkwardness.

Drawing himself up to his full height, clearing his throat, and looking solemnly into the faces of the other passengers, he intoned: "I suppose you're wondering why I called you all together!"

There was startled silence for just a moment, and then all the passengers burst into laughter. Larry Ward's quick wit again had asserted itself.

"Humor," Reinhold Niebuhr held, "is a prelude to faith,

and laughter is the beginning of prayer." But humor is only humor when the ridiculous, ironical, surprising, or ludicrous is recognized. Larry Ward moves easily from deep, genuine, hearty laughter to the reflective things of God and prayer.

Working in a world in which twenty-eight people starve to death every minute, constantly confronted with the heartbreaking dilemmas of human need, Larry finds a welcome change of pace in the humor which surrounds him on every side. He is quick to see it, eager to share it with others. In foreign lands where citizens are eager to use English, puns and non sequiturs and awkward phrases pop up to entertain and amuse. He quotes a road sign in Japan years ago, for example: "If a pedestrian of the foot hove in sight, tootle the horn." Or he relates the cable following a dramatic answer to prayer which was supposed to say "God reigns!" but somehow came out "God resigns!"

While at *Christian Life,* he once wrote an editorial based on a sign he had seen in the deep South of the United States. It was supposed to say "Meeting Place of the United Brethren." Nothing wrong with that, but some amateur sign painter had transposed two letters and it came out, "Meeting Place of the *Untied* Brethren." Larry's editorial made the obvious point.

"Thank God for a sense of humor," Larry says. "I think it has probably helped to keep me alive. In a miserable old world such as the one we live in, it would be pretty dismal if we couldn't enjoy a little humor. I have found that if I can make people laugh, probably no one is going to shoot me! If I act like a buffoon in the middle of the dangers, I do it on purpose much of the time. But I have to admit I also can't help it. That's my corny sense of humor."

Sometimes it is difficult to tell whether he thinks something is funny, or whether he is quoting it just because the idea that anyone would find it humorous is so absurd. For example, riding along in a car he is suddenly apt to speak up during a lull in the conversation, to have a quick dialogue with himself:

"My sister is going to marry an Irishman." "Oh, really?" "No—O'Reilly!"

"My brother's sick." "Oh, is he?" "No, Ikey!"

Or (perhaps even worse): "Did you hear about the bird that ran into the meat grinder?" Then, without waiting for an answer, "It came out shredded tweet!"

But sometimes his humor has practical value. Customs formalities around the world always seem to present Larry with a special challenge and opportunity to pit his skills and quick wit against oppressive bureaucracy. One time Larry arrived in Tokyo from Saigon with a very important load of film. On the other side of the customs door stood Yasushi Taguchi, Japanese producer, waiting to pick up the film and whisk it off to a laboratory. After a call from Saigon, he had agreed to work on the film that night, and then return it to Larry in the morning, so he could carry it to the United States for use on the Today show.

But Larry knew that he had a problem. There was nothing wrong with the film he carried, and no reason whatever why it should be detained in customs. But he was aware that a new policy had been invoked, and that all film coming into Japan was supposed to be inspected. This might take a full day—and Larry just didn't have that time to spend.

While he waited in the baggage claim area for his suitcase to be delivered, acutely aware of that big briefcase full of film at his feet, he entered into some friendly banter with a customs official standing over behind a desk. When Larry's suitcase arrived that man motioned for him to come over to his station. As Larry lifted his suitcase and that all-important briefcase to the table, the customs officer posed the usual question: "Anything to declare?"

Looking the man squarely in the eye, Larry said with great enthusiasm: "I declare—it's *great* to be back in Japan!"

The Japanese broke into a great roar of appreciative laughter, turning around to explain it to his colleagues—and at the same time waving Larry through.

On another occasion Larry and two of his colleagues arrived in Bangkok from Dhaka, Bangladesh. The daughter of one of the workers there had persuaded him to carry "a bit of furniture" for her. By the time it reached the Dhaka airport to accompany him and the others in the group to Bangkok, it had grown into a full living room of wicker furniture.

Again, there was nothing wrong in what Larry was doing—no customs violation. But he knew the situation well enough to know that it might be impounded, and he would have to spend all the next day trying to clear it. He didn't have that much time to spend, for he was due to leave in the early morning to go out to the refugee camps.

As his party moved up to the customs desk, Larry turned around and quickly whispered: "Whatever you do, don't laugh. Give me your passports, and if the man asks you anything, just answer in Spanish or Urdu or something. Leave it totally up to me."

The customs official blinked as the three thick passports were placed together on the counter before him. "Some sort of group?"

Propping his hand behind his ear as if he couldn't quite hear the question, Larry answered: "Singapore, Tuesday!"

No matter what the official asked, Larry kept repeating those same words: "Singapore—Tuesday!"

By this time the porters were beginning to deposit all the pieces of furniture in front of the counter. The already-bewildered official shook his head in wonderment: "What all this?"

Again Larry repeated, loudly: "Singapore—Tuesday!"

The customs official surrendered. No point talking to anyone who couldn't hear him. With a disgusted wave of the hand he sent the whole party—and all the furniture—through the door and out into the street.

The humor Larry appreciates most is not some attempt of his own to be funny, but the natural humor he sees in situations around him.

He and a group of friends had been discussing in Japan the tendency to confuse the "L" and "R," so that "dry cleaning," for example, may come out "dly creaning."

As the three neared a museum, Larry marveled at the beautiful poster outside—and the flawless English. Everything was fine, except the bottom line listing the museum hours said "Crosed Thursday."

Larry couldn't help breaking into laughter, and then was quickly embarrassed, for he didn't want to offend their Japanese friend.

"I don't mean to be rude in laughing," he said, "but you speak such good English that I knew you would see the humor to us in that bottom line, 'Crosed Thursday.'"

The Japanese friend looked and then began to laugh. "I get it! In United States you crose on Sundays!"

Larry was riding with his colleague Dulal Borpujari on a Thai International flight when a stewardess paused beside them and held out a tray. Neatly rolled up, looking somehow (to Larry, at least) like a row of white sausages, were a number of hot napkins. "Oh, no," said Larry, pretending to be offended, "I tried them once—and they tasted terrible!"

The stewardess looked quickly around, as if hoping no one had heard this stupid American. Then she bent down close to his ear and whispered politely, "Sir, they are not for eating. They are for washing the face."

"Oh, thank you," Larry said politely, surrendering on the spot.

Larry has apparently always been quick with his repartee. A high school chum recalls how his father had taken a group of Norwich High freshmen, Larry among them, to a football game at Syracuse University. As they neared the campus, the father mused, out loud and reflectively, "I wonder why it is that they always put colleges and universities on hills?" Immediately Larry responded: "Because these are institutions of *higher* learning!"

As we rode along in India one day in mid-1982, Larry

was extolling the virtues of country western music. (He defends it as "pure Americana," and insists that some of the most clever and colorful writing to be found anywhere today is pounded out by Nashville lyricists.) "All right, Larry," I challenged. "Write us a new country western song."

Instantly Larry broke into a nasal ballad, extending his arms to illustrate the dimensions of an imaginary love: "I love her more and more each day—thar's so much more to love!"

Another time, as we drove along in downtown Bangkok, I commented both on the abundance of massage facilities and the fact that they all seemed to be labeled with the same two words, "Massage Parlor." Larry nodded and quickly came up with two new advertising slogans. One was "Rubbing Kindness" and the other, "It's Nice to Feel Kneaded."

Roy Wolfe tells how he and Larry were at a Los Angeles Dodgers baseball game with Bob Pierce. Bob, who was also quick to note the unusual or the humorous in a situation, suddenly exclaimed: "Look, guys. Over there—three blind men coming up the stairs. I never saw a blind man at a ball game before. Why on earth would they come here?"

Larry instantly offered the only logical explanation. "They're umpires, on their day off."

Some years ago, while living in Hong Kong, Larry discovered that he is allergic to the serum in which cholera vaccine is packed. His British doctor tersely warned, "Quite serious. Could be fatal."

That to Larry sounded reasonably serious, but he was traveling constantly and knew that in many countries at that time the shot was required for entrance. "Write your own," snapped the doctor. "Fake it, as you Americans say. Better that than die."

Larry decided he had better obey doctor's orders, and since then has administered all his own cholera shots—with a fountain pen. I have checked Larry's yellow shot record card, however, and found that even here his irrepressible humor breaks through. His cholera shots bear the signature, "Marcus Welby, M.D."

During the last days of South Vietnam, as Dr. Garth Hunt and Larry were first beginning to launch the "exodus" in which Larry and Food for the Hungry eventually sponsored over eighteen hundred people, there were two occasions when Larry's ability to think fast saved the day.

Larry was standing at Tan Son Nhut airport, in the confusion of the evacuation center established by the U.S. military, holding his first list of sixty-two names and wondering just where to start.

Suddenly he heard the booming voice of an American colonel asking, "Where's the special group phone?"

Larry's ears perked up, and he watched as the colonel was directed to a special telephone nearby. Sliding as close as he dared, trying not to reveal that he was eavesdropping, Larry caught the drift of the man's conversation.

After the colonel had left, Larry stepped over and picked up the phone. "Ward here," he barked as soon as someone answered, trying to put as much authority as possible into his tone, "with the Food for the Hungry group."

"The *what?*"

"The Food for the Hungry group."

"I haven't heard of that one before!"

"Well, we're here," said Larry, "sixty-two of us. I've got 'em all stashed away in the old 'Dodge City' barracks." Without waiting for any further question he hurried on, "What's the procedure?"

"Well, I have to give you a number," said the other man, "and you must use it when you call in every hour or so. Then I'll tell you when you are scheduled to leave, and when you should take your group out to the planes. Let's see, sixty-two of you. . . ." And then, briskly, "O-kay—Food for the Hungry Special List sixty-two. F-H-S-L, sixty-two. Foxtrot hotel sierra lima sixty-two. That's your code. Got it?"

Larry had it, and that single swift action of his had probably saved hours of time trying to get official permission—and perhaps, ultimately, had saved those sixty-two lives and many more.

But there was one more unexpected hurdle to cross in the hours which followed. After making numerous calls to that mysterious voice on the special group phone (Larry never did find out the other person's name), each time using the code but updating the number as his initial list of sponsorees grew, Larry finally heard the welcomed instruction, "Take your group through the last gate in thirty minutes, and then someone out on the line will put you on the right plane."

Larry rushed back to "Dodge City," anxious to share the good news with his Vietnamese friends. But as he entered the barracks, he saw gloom and alarm written all over the face of one Vietnamese man, a former official in the Saigon city government.

"It won't work," said the man. "I showed our papers to the officer at the gate and asked if they were all right, and he said 'no.'"

Oh, no, thought Larry, *worst thing he could have done.* (Larry had provided each Vietnamese family with a form he had prepared, complete with the very official-looking red seal of Food for the Hungry's Vietnam incorporation. It wasn't exactly illegal. But it was rather unusual. It had been all he could do, though, and so far it had worked.)

The gloomy Vietnamese continued, "The man at the gate said we have to have the U.S. Embassy stamp."

Larry was furious, and the Vietnamese sensed it. "Oh, Mister Larry was *so* mad with me," the man laughingly recalled to Lorraine some months ago. "First he got red, and then he got white—and I think finally he turned green."

The man wasn't far off. Larry Ward was furious. This man's nervous "jumping the gun" might have destroyed the whole plan. This was no time to raise a question in anyone's mind. But fortunately the officer who had expressed this negative opinion had just left, and now a big Black

American sergeant was standing all alone at the gate.

Larry recalls: "I didn't have the slightest idea what to say to the sergeant. I had the most profound respect for those American G.I.s, doing a great job at a most difficult time, and I didn't want to get him in trouble. Also, if I tried to explain and made it all sound too complicated, he would have to send for the lieutenant—and that could blow the whole thing. Believe me, I was praying!"

By faith Larry ordered his Vietnamese group to go outside and line up, and then he walked toward the gate.

Reaching the G.I., still not knowing where to begin, Larry opened his mouth, and somehow the words tumbled out: "Sarge, I need your help. I've got ninety-four people lined up over there beside that truck—in a 'column of twos.' They are ready to come through this gate, but I want to make sure I've got exactly the right number. If there are more than ninety-four, I've got some 'ringer' or 'ringers' in there who don't belong, and we don't want that, do we?"

The sergeant shook his head emphatically. "No, sir!"

"And sarge, if there are less than ninety-four, I may be leaving somebody behind—and that would be worse, wouldn't it?"

"Yes, sir—can't have that happen!"

"Sarge, will you help me count them?"

He nodded his quick assent, and then stepped out to sweep his big hand through the air and beckon the group toward the gate. "Move 'em out," he bellowed.

Staring straight ahead, for they knew how critical this moment was, Larry's little band of Vietnamese marched through the gate. As they walked past, Larry and the sergeant were counting in unison. "Two, four, six" and so on up to "eighty-eight, ninety, ninety-two and—"

"Ninety-four!" shouted the sergeant triumphantly.

"Ninety-four!" echoed Larry, tossing the G.I. a happy and very grateful salute.

And then Larry added, as the gate closed behind his greatly relieved Vietnamese friends, "I'll have other groups coming through, sarge—some smaller, some larger."

"Will I have to count them?" asked sarge, helpfully.

"Naw," replied Larry, *not as long as they have these papers.*" And he held out a sample document for the G.I. to see, complete with the red corporate seal of Food for the Hungry.

One of the members of that group of ninety-four was Larry's Montagnard friend Ha Jimmy. He recalls: "We were all so frightened as we walked through that gate and Dr. Ward and the sergeant counted. But then we knew the Lord had helped us. So we walked on around a building out of sight and formed a circle. Even the ones who were not Christians seemed to know what to do. I said, 'Let us pray,' and then I thanked the Lord for our deliverance."

Larry sums it up: "When I remember that scene, or when someone else tells about it, on the surface it sounds kinda funny. But remember—I didn't have the faintest idea of what to say. I'm not that smart. I just prayed, and then I opened my mouth and the words came out. This was another wonderful time when 'this poor man cried—and the Lord heard him'!"

twenty-three
BEYOND TODAY

How do you sum up a life like this? One way is to listen to Larry's own words.

Not long ago, he sat down in front of a video camera in the Scottsdale offices of Food for the Hungry and quietly filmed a brief message to be played at his own funeral.

"I realize that this is a bit unusual," Larry began, "and I don't want to make anyone uncomfortable, or to add to the grief of those whom I have loved so much and from whom I am now separated by that grim curtain of death. But I have a very special reason for doing this, and somehow I dare to trust that you all will understand.

"Yes, I have been to a few other funerals in my life, and I recognize the natural tendency is to want to say good things about the dear departed.

"That's why I felt I should add a few words of my own, just to set the record straight.

"I have prepared another very personal tape for my dear family, so I am not particularly addressing myself to them at this time.

"I just want you all to know that if there has been anything of real and lasting value in this one man's life, it's because *God was there* when I needed him.

"I think you sense that this is a time when a man has to choose his words very carefully. He has to be 'dead-level' honest, if you will pardon the expression. And that's what I am endeavoring to do right now.

"The most important thing I ever did in my life was to accept the Lord Jesus Christ as my personal Savior. He has made all the difference in my life, and I urge you—oh yes, *I urge you*—to come to know and trust him as I have. When you come to the end of your life, as I have now in mine, you will realize that this is the most important decision in life.

"When Jesus comes into your life, you will have *everything you need* to prepare you for whatever comes. You'll have his Word to come alive and give you guidance—his Holy Spirit to give you the power to obey and follow the directions of this wonderful book, the Holy Bible. Yes, I urge you—right now, today, even here—to accept Jesus Christ as your Lord and Savior.

"And as I look back over the many years since I first came to know him, I realize that the only things of *lasting* value in my life are those things which *he* did.

"I'm sure I disappointed him many times in my life—but he has never disappointed me. He has never let me down.

"All that I have done, through all these years and all around the world, is to cry out to him for help. I can't take any credit, but I'm glad that I at least had sense enough to realize how much I needed him.

"I thank God for the privilege of being a hand to help the hungry, these many years. They're still out there—the hungry and hurting and homeless—but now I have to leave them with you who remain. You see, with the psalmist I now can say (using the words of Psalm 81) that I have heard the voice which said, 'Now I will relieve your shoulder of its burden; I will free your hands from their heavy tasks' (v. 6). And I like the next verse, where God reminds: 'You cried to me in trouble and I saved you.'

"Thank you for your kind thoughts today—and I suppose

I should say thanks for the nice words that friends have wanted to say about me.

"But here where I am—where truth prevails and truth is all that matters—let me sum it up in these words: 'To God be the glory; great things *he* has done.' 'This poor man cried—and the Lord heard him!'"

THE WHITE HOUSE

WASHINGTON

May 7, 1984

Dear Larry:

Individuals of great goodness and humanity seldom receive the recognition due them, and you are no exception. For over 25 years, you have worked tirelessly to relieve the suffering of the homeless, the hungry and the victims of disaster and war. You have created international bridges between peoples with a simple humanitarian appeal -- help the poor.

Your good works, your sincerity and your consistent and constant message shine as a beacon of hope that mankind can be noble and good. There is little we can do adequately to recognize such accomplishment, but I hope you will accept my personal designation as our Honorary Ambassador to the Hungry World.

As you step down from the Presidency of Food for the Hungry International, I know it does not mean the end of your good works, for your work is obviously a way of life. You make us all proud to be fellow Americans. May God bless you and your family.

Sincerely,

Ronald Reagan

This poor man cried . . .
and the Lord heard him
and saved him
out of his troubles.
PSALM 34:6 (TLB)

He listened
and heard my cry.
PSALM 40:1 (TLB)

from the last page of
Larry Ward's Bible

For more information, write:

Food for the Hungry, Inc.
Headquarters:
7729 East Greenway Road
Scottsdale, Arizona 85260
Phone: (602) 998-3100